Praise for *Luther for Everyone*

This short book is a robust account of Martin Luther as a prophetic teacher of the whole church whose influence extends beyond the sixteenth century and the confines of the church that bears his name. Hans Schwarz condenses his considerable knowledge of Luther and Reformation research into a lively and accessible narrative of key themes in the reformer's theology and the author's suggestions for applications today. Beyond these traditional topics, Schwarz includes an engaging chapter on Luther's rejection of astrology and another on how Luther's theology is open to science.

—John T. Pless, assistant professor of pastoral ministry
and missions, Concordia Theological Seminary,
Fort Wayne, Indiana

With approachable erudition, Hans Schwarz shows how Martin Luther's theology impacts our culture in more ways than people may initially think. It behooves non-Lutherans and even secular people to know its basics. The author models how to appropriate Luther's wisdom for contemporary people: Schwarz's Luther engages with public concerns such as economic and social inequities as well as the increasing role of science in our lives. Much Luther scholarship is done in a bubble isolated from real-life concerns. Schwarz bursts this bubble.

—Mark Mattes, department chair in theology,
Grand View University, Des Moines, Iowa

Prof. Hans Schwarz has done an enormous favor to everyone, both Lutherans and non-Lutherans, with this extraordinarily clear introduction to what Martin Luther has done not just for Lutheran Christians but for all Christians. I would venture to claim that he has done this for those who stayed away from the Christian worldview. Karl Jaspers used to stress to his students the importance of "communication" rather than "interpretation" of texts or thinkers: Hans Schwarz has done exactly that with clear communication so that everyone can understand, and even be persuaded and convinced of, what Luther has achieved. Furthermore, everyone who reads this book will have a deeper understanding of the Christian culture and value orientation.

This is a remarkable achievement, worthy of being recognized with other notable Luther books (such as Heinz Schilling's recent *Martin Luther: Rebel in an Age of Upheaval*). Uncommonly entertaining, the book is peppered with acute observations and unexpected comparisons that clarify and enlighten Luther's positions. Required reading for serious students and laypersons looking for a clear historical and theological narrative of the legacy of Luther and the place of his legacy in the blurry world of religious pluralism. I strongly recommend this to everyone.

—Dr. Young Ho Chun, professor emeritus of systematic theology, Saint Paul School of Theology

LUTHER
for
EVERYONE

LUTHER
for
EVERYONE

Who He Was & Why He Still Matters

Hans Schwarz

FORTRESS PRESS
MINNEAPOLIS

Hans Schwarz, *Luther für Nichtlutheraner* © 2021 Brill Ferdinand Schöningh
Translated from the German by Hans Schwarz

Library of Congress Control Number: 2023031130 (print)

Cover image: Luther Triumphant Des Ehrwirdigen Herrn Doctoris Martini
Lutheri, gottseligen, Triumph, und Verantwortung, wider die gottlosen
Schmehschrifft, der newenMünch, der Jesuiter, welche sie vnter dem Titel,
Anatomia Lutheri, ausgesprenget haben. Wittenberg: [s.n., 1568]. The image
provided courtesy of Pitts Theology Library, Candler School of Theology,
Emory University
Cover design: Laurie Ingram

Print ISBN: 978-1-5064-9830-0
eBook ISBN: 978-1-5064-9831-7

Contents

Preface   vii

Introduction   ix

Abbreviations   xv

1. The Basic Principles of Lutheran Faith   1

2. The Initiator of a Worldwide Reformation   11

3. "By Grace Alone": A Unique Feature
   of the Lutherans?   25

4. God Is Unfathomable   39

5. The Gospel Is Not a Law   61

6. The Two Ways in Which God Rules   73

7. Education Is for Everybody   93

8. A Calling Is Not Just for Priests   109

9. Watching How People Speak   125

10. Against Predatory Capitalism   133

11. The Christian Faith Is Not Hostile to Science   151

12. Astrology Does Not Give Us a Glimpse
    into the Future   157

CONTENTS

13. Against Patriarchalism   167

14. A Church Service Must Be Joyful   185

15. Martin Luther: Heretic, Saint, or Reformer?   201

    Selected Bibliography   209

Preface

Don't we already have enough books about Martin Luther? On the five hundredth anniversary of the publication of Luther's Ninety-Five Theses of 1517 alone, dozens of books on the Reformer came onto the market. Now comes a book about Martin Luther for readers who do not come from the Lutheran tradition. Well, the idea for such a book did not come from me but from Martin Illert from the Roman Catholic Schöningh Verlag. For those interested in Luther, there are truly enough books. But for readers who hardly know Luther or have nothing to do with him at all, this is not the case. So, I was happy to take up the idea, as the Reformer Martin Luther has become influential far beyond the Lutheran church. Luther was not just a reformer of what later became the Lutheran wing of the Reformation. He was a public figure whose immense influence went far beyond the Lutherans and the Reformation. Just as an example: when the then-Catholic city of Regensburg and the bishop of Regensburg were quarrelling with each other over who would get the revenue from the then-popular pilgrimage to pray at the feet of the Beautiful Virgin Mary of Regensburg, the city council asked Martin Luther for an opinion who should receive the money.

It came as no surprise that Pope John Paul II explicitly addressed Martin Luther and the Reformation on each of his three pastoral trips to Germany. In most countries Christians live in denominationally mixed areas, so actually Protestants should of course know something about Roman Catholicism and its leading convictions, and in return Roman Catholics should know about what is important for Protestants. But the Reformer Martin Luther is often largely unknown to Catholics and even to some Protestants, and therefore he is often still somewhat suspect. In order to clear up misunderstandings, a better knowledge of the Reformer is helpful.

The following pages do not want to defend Martin Luther and his concerns, but they are intended to show in understandable language what we still owe to the Reformer today in church and society. That he had an impact far beyond the ecclesiastical space is often forgotten or shortened to catchy topics such as "Luther and the Jews." However, Luther was not a saint and, like every human being, had his weaknesses. This should not be ignored, although this is not the main focus of this book. The focus is on his service to the Christian faith and to society.

I would like to thank Will Bergkamp and Ryan Hemmer from Fortress Press for making possible this publication, which first appeared in the German with Schöningh Verlag. I would like to thank Andrea Bauer from my former chair at the University of Regensburg for her help in obtaining relevant literature. Last but not least, I want to thank my wife for letting me again work undisturbed in my study, even though I had promised her that I would not write another book so quickly so that we would finally have more time for each other.

Hans Schwarz
Regensburg, Summer 2022

Introduction

Why should a Roman Catholic or an Orthodox believer care about Martin Luther? For Catholics, didn't Luther cause the Catholic Church severe problems that led to a split of the church in the West? For the Orthodox, Luther is largely a foreign entity, and vice versa. Although Luther appreciated the councils of the early church and adhered to their doctrinal decisions, the Orthodox church structures, with patriarchs, archbishops, and metropolitans, as well as the veneration of icons, played no role for Luther. Why, then, Luther for non-Lutherans?

This reminds me of an episode during my student days. Since I studied English literature in addition to theology, I had to acquire some certificates in French. In the French language course, such expressions as "altar," "corpus Christi," and "host" were also used. Some fellow students protested that one would probably not have to learn such a vocabulary if one had nothing to do with the church. But the lecturer, Mrs. Zöbelein, replied that they had to be learned very well, because they were part of general education. Thus, a basic knowledge of Martin Luther and his most important statements belongs to the general education of non-Lutherans, as also applies to the knowledge of Thomas Aquinas and Karl Rahner for Lutherans and other Protestants.

I remember an educated Greek Orthodox abbot, a good friend of mine, who once asked me, "Hans, do you [Lutherans] also have sacraments?" When I explained to him that we have two sacraments, baptism and the Lord's Supper, but also other rites, such as marriage, confirmation, ordination, and so on, which we do not call sacraments but consider very important, he said, "It's almost like with us." Ignorance of other denominations often leads to prejudices and deepens the rifts between denominations. Therefore, it is important for non-Lutherans to know what this Luther is all about. Was he really a heretic and a church divider from whom one should stay as far away as possible?

Even if you are not interested in this as a non-Lutheran, it is not so easy to escape Luther and his Reformation. He has had such a broad impact that its effects are visible even where one does not suspect them at all. This was evident at the five hundredth anniversary of Martin Luther's Ninety-Five Theses, an event that was commemorated worldwide in 2017, following a ten-year so-called Luther decade. From 2008 to 2016, this decade invited visitors to search for traces of Luther and the Reformation at important original locations with a variety of events and travel offers. Throughout Germany, exhibitions, concerts, and other cultural events were dedicated to the various aspects of the Reformation. Each year had a different motto, such as "Reformation and Freedom" (2011), "Reformation and Music" (2012), and "Reformation and Politics" (2014).

Because Luther came to Wittenberg for the first time in autumn 1508, the city that was to become his most important place of work, the Luther decade was solemnly opened in the castle church at Wittenberg. Since Luther had come to Wittenberg as a monk, as was customary in the sixteenth century, by barge across the Elbe, on September 20, 2008, a figure representing Luther crossed the Elbe with a barge and was solemnly welcomed by citizens and guests of the city. Part of the opening event was also the beginning of a Luther Garden, in which churches from all over the world, Lutheran and non-Lutheran, could sponsor one of the five hundred trees that were to be planted there. This was intended as a symbol of the worldwide impact of the Reformation as well as of the solidarity, networking, and reconciliation of the Christian churches worldwide.

In contrast to earlier Reformation celebrations, the aim was to place the unity and reconciliation of the Christian churches at the center of the celebrations and not the differences between Lutherans and Catholics. That was why people often spoke of a Reformation commemoration instead of a Reformation celebration. The five hundredth anniversary of Martin Luther's Ninety-Five Theses was therefore no longer understood as a Lutheran event from which Catholics distanced themselves, but as an anniversary that appealed to both Lutherans and Roman Catholics, and also to non-Lutherans. While denominational demarcation and self-assertion were the order of the day in the sixteenth century, five hundred years later it was a matter of bridging confessional differences. This was not simply am attempt to undo the past and sweep it under the carpet but to see the past in its former context and wonder whether this context was still relevant and valid for us today.

For example, in the minutes of the first meeting of the Joint Ecumenical Commission, which met in Munich, Germany, on May 6–7, 1981, we read: "Cardinal Ratzinger thought that a corresponding reexamination of doctrinal decisions of the Council of Trent was also necessary. It was important to formulate here, which is always presupposed in Protestant-Catholic dialogue: that new realities have come into being, and that the old massive dissensus to all intents and purposes no longer exists."[1] At this first meeting of the commission, which was constituted following the visit of Pope John Paul II to Germany, it became clear that the judgments of the sixteenth century that one church passed on another, which were then incorporated into the confessional writings of the Lutheran and Reformed churches or into the doctrinal decisions of the Council of Trent, were outdated. "According to the general conviction, these so-called condemnations no longer apply to our partner today."[2] As early as 1983, Roman Catholic theologian Peter Manns (1923–1991), at a series of lectures staged by the Institute for European History at Mainz on the occasion of Martin Luther's five hundredth birthday,

1 Karl Lehmann and Wolfhart Pannenberg, eds., *The Condemnations of the Reformation Era: Do They Still Divide?*, trans. Margaret Kohl (Minneapolis: Fortress, 1990), 168.

2 Lehmann and Pannenberg, *Condemnations of the Reformation Era*, 169.

called Luther "'father of faith' for the whole of Christendom."[3] His principles of faith—Christ alone, Scripture alone, grace alone, and faith alone—are also the principles of faith for the whole of Christendom. Luther never left the one church, nor did he want to found his own church.

On October 31, 1999, that is, Reformation Day, the "Historical Joint Declaration on the Doctrine of Justification" was signed in Augsburg, Germany, by Roman Catholics (Cardinal Edward Idris Cassidy and Bishop Walter Kasper) and Lutherans (Christian Krause, bishop and president of the Lutheran World Federation; Ishmael Noko, Lutheran World Federation general secretary; and six vice presidents of the Lutheran World Federation). The preamble to the declaration points out that, from a Reformation point of view, the core of all disputes consisted in a different understanding of the doctrine of justification, namely, how is a sinful human being reconciled to God? In the Lutheran confessional writings and in the Council of Trent, opposing statements were made about this doctrine, which are still valid today and have a church-dividing effect. On the basis of the previous dialogue between the Catholic and Lutheran churches, it was now officially established that there was "a consensus on basic truths of the doctrine of justification" and "that the remaining differences in its explication are no longer the occasion for doctrinal condemnations."[4] There was now official agreement on the essential points of the doctrine of justification. Pope John Paul II was therefore right when he noted during his visit to Germany in 1996 that rifts had been bridged "that previous generations considered unbridgeable. This progress has become possible because methodically careful care has been taken to distinguish

---

3 So Peter Manns in his thoughtful essay, "Was macht Martin Luther zum 'Vater des Glaubens' für die eine Christenheit?," in *Martin Luther "Reformator und Vater im Glauben": Referate aus der Vortragsreihe des Instituts für Europäische Geschichte Mainz*, ed. Peter Manns (Wiesbaden: Steiner, 1985), 15.

4 "Declaration on the Doctrine of Justification," October 31, 1999, preamble, 5, https://tinyurl.com/mr2p3uee.

between the content of faith itself and the formulation in which it is expressed."[5]

So, it is not enough to compare certain statements with each other; at the same time, one has to ask what is meant by these statements. One really has to get to know the dialogue partner so that one can determine the content of the similarities and differences. Thus, it makes sense, or is perhaps even necessary, that non-Lutherans inform themselves about Martin Luther, because even Roman Catholics are no longer separated by anything essential from this pioneer of a worldwide Reformation. So, what were and still are the basic principles of Lutheran faith? Are these really foreign to other beliefs, such as those of Roman Catholic or Reformed believers?

---

5 Address by John Paul II to the representatives of the Evangelical Church and the Association of Christian Churches in Germany, Paderborn, 1996, https://tinyurl.com/mtawn3uy.

Abbreviations

LW   *Luther's Works: American Edition.* Vols. 1–30 edited by Jaroslav Pelikan. Vols. 31–54 edited by Helmut T. Lehmann. Vols. 56– edited by Christopher Boyd Brown. St. Louis: Concordia; Philadelphia: Fortress, 1955–1967; St. Louis: Concordia, 1968–.

WA   *D. Martin Luthers Werke: Kritische Gesamtausgabe; Schriften,* 73 vols. Weimar: Hermann Böhlaus Nachfolger, 1883–2009.

WA BR   *D. Martin Luthers Werke: Kritische Gesamtausgabe; Briefwechsel.* 18 vols. Weimar: Hermann Böhlaus Nachfolger. 1930–1985.

WA DB   *D. Martin Luthers Werke: Kritische Gesamtausgabe: Die Deutsche Bibel.* 12 vols. Weimar: Hermann Böhlaus Nachfolger, 1906–1961.

WA TR   *D. Martin Luthers Werke: Kritische Gesamtausgabe; Tischreden.* 6 vols. Weimar: Hermann Böhlaus Nachfolger, 1912–1921.

CHAPTER ONE

The Basic Principles of Lutheran Faith

A few years ago, a young man from Korea did his doctorate with me. When the end of his successful doctoral studies was foreseeable, I asked him which denomination he would join after his return. He had only recently been converted to Christianity through his studies in Korea and had not yet joined a specific denomination. He replied, "It is not important to belong to a certain denomination. Rather, it is crucial to be a Christian." Of course, it is crucial to be a Christian. But especially in Korea, it is also important to belong to a denomination, because without such an affiliation one cannot teach in a theological institution there. I replied, "It's not that simple, because every denomination has a certain view of the gospel from which it understands the Christian faith." Since I knew the Lutheran church in Korea fairly well, I suggested that he become a Lutheran. After some hesitation, he agreed. After appropriate preparation, he was confirmed, and after passing the conditions for admission to the Lutheran church in Korea, he became a pastor.

Every denomination presents a particular view of the gospel. Since the Lutheran church, like the Roman Catholic Church, belongs to Western Christianity, the Latin language emphasizes the juridical language. In the Catholic Church this is reflected by the high importance of canon law, and in the Lutheran church by the emphasis on justification. While the Catholic Church emphasizes that all believers follow the precepts of canon law and that the pope ultimately has the primacy of jurisdiction, the Lutheran church emphasizes that God justifies the believer through God's undeserved grace. Eastern Christianity is shaped by the Greek mind, and the goal of believers is deification, that is, the complete penetration of the faithful by the Spirit of God. In Orthodoxy, justification by which one is received by God by grace alone plays a lesser role.

1. THE CONFESSIONS ARE GUIDELINES FOR THE FAITH

The Lutheran church is a confessional church. This distinguishes it from churches that consciously reject any Christian confession, such as the Apostles' Creed, or confessional writings, with the claim that confessions have always led to divisions in the church. For example, in 1881 the Church of God (Anderson, Indiana) was founded and it based its teachings on the Bible only. The denomination wanted to overcome church divisions and unite all those for whom the Bible, as the inspired word of God, was the foundation of their faith. However, the Church of God, which today has over a million members, published a confession on its one hundredth anniversary (*We Believe*, published by Anderson University School of Theology) so that people would know what Christians believe in this church. In the long run, one cannot do without a confession as a summary of one's own faith, because the Bible can be read very differently—liberal, conservative, or fundamentalist. A confession as expressed in *The Book of Concord: The Confessional Writings of the Evangelical Lutheran Church* is a point of reference for faith to which one can refer. For example, at the Imperial Diet of Augsburg in 1530, the Augsburg Confession (*Confessio Augustana*) was read to the emperor to show that Lutherans had not deviated from the right faith. After almost five hundred years, this confession is still a guideline for Lutherans on how to understand the biblically based faith.

Confessions, whether the Apostles' Creed or the Augsburg Confession, are only guidelines for a Lutheran, not the norm for the Christian faith. The norm is sacred Scripture alone, and everything else, including confessions, must be checked again and again to see whether it is scriptural. Thus, the Lutheran confessional writings state, "We believe, teach and confess that the only rule and guiding principle according to which all teachings and teachers are to be evaluated and judged are the prophetic and apostolic writings of the Old and New Testaments alone."[1]

For Martin Luther, Scripture was the unquestionable norm of the Christian faith. But the text of the Bible is not uniform. It includes poetry (the Psalms), epistles (Paul), laws (purity laws in the OT), and narratives (the exodus from Egypt). Luther judged that the Old Testament law was "the *Sachsenspiegel* of the Jews," that is, a law that was primarily mandatory for the Israelites, but it is not a binding norm for Christians.[2] He therefore distinguished in the Bible between the center (which inspires the Christian faith) and the periphery (which has little or nothing to do with Christ). Overall, however, all biblical writings testify to God's self-disclosure in history.

Since the biblical writings are so different from each other and were composed on very different occasions, we must first grasp them in their respective historical contexts in order to understand them correctly. Thus, we must not tear a scriptural word out of the context in which it stands and immediately apply it to the present or freely combine it with other scriptural words from other historical contexts. The Bible is not a crossword puzzle but always wants to be understood contextually. However, it confronts us with the claim that it is God's word. So it is not a book like any other.

---

1 "The Formula of Concord (The Epitome)," in *The Book of Concord: The Confessions of the Evangelical Lutheran Church*, ed. Robert Kolb and Timothy J. Wengert (Minneapolis: Fortress, 2000), 486.

2 Martin Luther, "Against the Heavenly Prophets in the Matters of Images and Sacraments" (1525), *LW* 40:98.

2. THE DISTINCTION BETWEEN
LAW AND GOSPEL

The Bible is first and foremost a book that speaks to us as law and/or gospel. On the one hand, it confronts us with the God who shows us, as Luther once wrote in a song, that "No strength of ours can match his might! We would be lost, rejected."[3] The more we think about our life, the more we realize that we are not the way we want to be. In other words, we are sinners. This is already evident in the first commandment, where God says, "I am the LORD your God, . . . you shall have no other gods before me" (Exod 20:1–2). But how often is something or someone more important to us than God! Thus, this commandment is a law that shows us our estrangement from God, our sinfulness.

However, if one emphasizes the first part of this commandment and not the second, then this commandment loses its character as a law and becomes a wonderful promise: "I am the Lord your God." We are not alone and abandoned by God in this world, but God is our Lord and protector. The first commandment has been transformed into a great gospel. Therefore, we cannot divide the biblical words into those that contain law and others that contain the gospel. The Bible always speaks to us in two ways, exposing our sinful alienation from God, and when we are frightened by it and want to amend our ways, it shows us how God graciously turns to us. In sermons, it is important that law and gospel are strictly distinguished, that is, that the sermon does not slip into moralism. On the other hand, by concealing the law, cheap grace may be preached, according to either the motto, "We all go to heaven because we have tried so hard," or the vain idea, "God will forgive us, because that's what God is there for." No, God is God, was the insight of Luther, and not a figure who spreads the cloak of cheap grace over everything we do. That is why the true fright of who we are is just as much a part of preaching the

---

3 Martin Luther, "A Mighty Fortress Is Our God," in *Evangelical Lutheran Worship* (Minneapolis: Augsburg Fortress, 2006), 503, stanza 2.

word of God as the comforting encouragement of the gospel. We are sinners and justified at the same time, and thus free children of God and not people who must constantly be held in check with the raised moral index finger.

The distinction between law and gospel continues in the so-called doctrine of the two regiments, namely, in the conviction that God governs the world in two different ways, in the kingdom on the left by the law, and in the kingdom on the right by the gospel. Here law is to be understood as the civil law by which order is maintained in the world, and disorder and evil are resisted. Everyone is subject to this law, whether Christian or non-Christian. Reference is made here to Romans 13, where Paul emphasizes that secular authority is ordained by God and must be obeyed. For this reason, the Lutherans were often accused of being subservient to the authorities. Reformed theologian Karl Barth (1886–1968) emphasized exactly the opposite of obedience to authority. First, he concedes a certain tension between church and state, saying, "The fact that the Church has had to assume a 'certain' political character is balanced by the fact that the Church must recognize and honor a 'certain' ecclesiastical character of the State." But then he continues, "The real Church must be the model and prototype of the real State."[4] But does not this overestimate the regulatory possibilities of the gospel? In addition to Romans 13, one must not forget Revelation 13, where worldly power is portrayed as a demonic seductive power. Thus, Lutheran theologian Walter Künneth (1901–1997), who wrote *Christian Ethics of Politics* (*Christliche Ethik des Politischen*) after the Second World War, rightly gave it the subtitle *Politics between the Demonic and God* (*Politik zwischen Dämon und Gott*). Many Christians did not recognize the seductive demonic skills of the National Socialists in time and thought that the National Socialists were an authority willed by God. On the other hand, many resistance fighters in the Third Reich were Lutherans,

---

4 Karl Barth, "The Christian Community and the Civil Community," in *Community, State and Church: Three Essays* (Gloucester, MA: Peter Smith, 1968), 134, 186.

such as Dietrich Bonhoeffer and Hans von Dohnanyi, who discerned that God did not legitimate such an authority. Luther himself always emphasized that in this world two kingdoms are at war with each other, the kingdom of evil and the kingdom of God.

What about the kingdom on the right, where God rules with the gospel? It was clear to Luther that no one should rule over our hearts, neither a prince nor a pope, but God alone. However, one must not equate the kingdom on the left with the state and the kingdom on the right with the church, because both in the state and in the church there are binding orders that one must follow. Many years ago, when I was teaching in a Lutheran theological seminary in the United States, a student did not want to write the obligatory term paper. When I explained to him that if he did not write a term paper, he would not pass the course, he replied, "Is there no grace here?" I replied, "No, even in a theological seminary there are certain rules that apply to everyone."

We cannot simply lead the church with the gospel, just as it is not possible to govern the state with the gospel, even if enthusiasts have tried to do so again and again. Since there are sinful people in the world, the world cannot do without laws, whose observance must be ensured according to certain rules that ensure a peaceful coexistence of everyone. Christians are called on to help so that order is maintained in all areas of life and no unjust order spreads.

3. "CHRIST ALONE" ALSO APPLIES TO THE SACRAMENTS

Another peculiarity of the Lutheran church is its understanding of the sacraments. The Roman Catholic Church at the Council of Trent (1545–1563), in contrast to the Reformation churches, stipulated that there were seven sacraments—baptism, confirmation, Eucharist, marriage, priestly ordination, penance and anointing of the sick. The

Reformed church in the Heidelberg Catechism of 1563 claimed that there were two sacraments, baptism and the Lord's Supper. But the Lutheran church has never committed itself to a certain number. In his *Large Catechism* Luther writes of "our two sacraments, instituted by Christ," but Philipp Melanchthon (1497–1560) defines baptism, the Lord's Supper, and absolution (the sacrament of repentance) "as rites, which have the command of God and to which the promise of grace is added."[5] They are sacraments, properly speaking. He could even call the preaching ministry—that is, priestly ordination—a sacrament.

This shows that the number of sacraments depends on what they are understood to be. If we understand them, with Luther, as appointed by Christ, we arrive at two sacraments. If we trace them back, with Melanchthon, to God's command, then even three or four spiritual acts can be called sacraments. If we also pay attention to tradition, we come to seven sacraments. In the early days of the church, the concept of sacraments was much broader than it was in the Reformation period, and sometimes over thirty sacraments were obtained. According to the Lutheran understanding, sacraments are visible signs of the invisible grace of God instituted by Christ. Here the Lutherans also differ from Pentecostal and evangelical denominations, which often avoid the term "sacrament," since this term sounds Roman Catholic to them. For them, the Lord's Supper is largely a remembrance of Christ's sacrificial death, and baptism is a confession of allegiance of the baptized person to Jesus Christ. This emphasizes our actions and not what God has done for us in Jesus Christ. For Lutherans, however, the focus is on God's actions in Jesus Christ. This is also reflected in the importance of Jesus Christ in the understanding of faith.

---

5 Martin Luther, *The Large Catechism*, in Kolb and Wengert, *Book of Concord*, 456; Philipp Melanchthon, "Apology of the Augsburg Confession," in Kolb and Wengert, *Book of Concord*, 219.

"Christ alone" was Martin Luther's watchword, not the pope or tradition. For Luther, Christ "is a mirror of the Father's heart."[6] In this way, we can detect from Christ how God relates to us. Christ is the human face of God, because "the humanity is that holy ladder of ours, mentioned in Genesis 28:12, by which we ascend to the knowledge of God."[7] Therefore, Lutherans naturally confess, with the Council of Chalcedon (451), that Jesus Christ is truly human and true God. Jesus Christ must be completely and wholly God. Otherwise he would not have been able to mediate God to us. At the same time, Christ had to be completely and wholly a human being. Otherwise he would not have been able to reach us and identify with us. From this insight, everything that is conveyed by the pope or tradition with regard to our faith must also be judged, because, according to Luther, "What Christ does not teach is not apostolic even if it were taught by Peter or Paul. Again, what Christ preaches is apostolic even if Judas, Hannah, Pilate, and Herod preached the same."[8]

With this emphasis on Christ, there follows a natural ecumenical orientation of Lutherans. They can enter into dialogue with all denominations and agree with them on many things, as long as the dialogue partner does not endanger that Jesus Christ is at the center of faith, as attested by the writings of the Old and New Testaments. Human traditions can always be agreed on, because, according to Luther, "Holiness does not consist of surplices, [. . . but] in the Word of God and true faith."[9] The Lutheran church should never forget that Luther wanted to reform a church that was in danger of letting Jesus Christ as its cornerstone fall into oblivion. This Reformation concern must be preserved today by the four Lutheran characteristics—Christ alone, Scripture alone, grace alone, and faith alone.

6 Luther, "Large Catechism," 440.

7 Martin Luther, "Lecture on Hebrews (1517/18)," comment on Heb 1:2 (*LW* 29:111).

8 Martin Luther, "Preface to the Letter of James (1522)," in *Prefaces to the New Testament* (*WA DB* 7:384.25–32).

9 Martin Luther, "Smalcald Articles," in Kolb and Wengert, *Book of Concord*, 325.

QUESTIONS FOR DISCUSSION

What has been your experience of creeds, confessions, and other summaries of faith? Do they have value in living and professing Christianity?

How has the idea of "the Law" impacted how you view the relationship between church and state?

How does the Lutheran view of sacraments differ that of both from other Protestants and Roman Catholics?

CHAPTER TWO

The Initiator of a Worldwide Reformation

As the main location for Martin Luther as a Reformer, Wittenberg was actually unsuitable. Its university had been founded only in 1502, by the Elector Frederick the Wise (1463–1525), and the city was, as Luther said in 1532, on the edge of civilization: if you go just one step further, then you are deep in barbarism. But in autumn 1508, surprisingly, Luther was sent by his order to Wittenberg to teach moral philosophy in the Faculty of Arts. Luther finally accepted a call to Wittenberg in 1511, and after completing his doctorate in theology in 1512, he assumed a professorship for biblical exegesis in the theological faculty of the university. He held this professorship until his death in 1546. Luther thus lived and worked on the edge of civilization and had visited only once a foreign country, namely, Italy, when he, together with an Augustinian monk from Nuremberg, was sent to Rome in 1510 by his order to present some problems.

Similar to philosopher Immanuel Kant, who had never left Königsberg, Luther did not live or work in isolation. On the one hand, this was due to his prince, since Frederick the Wise promoted his new university as the state university of his electorate. It developed into one of the most important universities in the German Empire. On the other hand, Martin Luther was so productive in literary ventures that he influenced many contemporaries and was in correspondence with many important personalities. If we take only a brief look at Luther's influence in Bohemia, England, and Scandinavia as examples, we should not think that his Reformation ideas were unknown in other regions. For instance, while the dukes of Bavaria closed themselves off to the Reformation, there were followers of Luther in many cities in Bavaria and some also in the countryside, where they usually were forced to revoke their new faith. Nevertheless, much to the displeasure of the Bavarian dukes, individual territorial lords introduced Luther's teachings in traditional Bavarian regions, such as the dukes of Palatinate-Neuburg, the counts of Haag, and the counts of Ortenburg.

1. LUTHER'S INFLUENCE IN BOHEMIA, ENGLAND, AND SCANDINAVIA

Luther was branded as a Hussite at the Leipzig Disputation of 1519 by his opponent, Ingolstadt professor Johannes Eck (1486–1543), though he was largely ignorant of Hussite teachings. Luther reported on July 20, 1519, to Electoral Saxon court preacher and secretary Georg Spalatin (1484–1545) that Eck "was holding the Bohemians before me and publicly accusing me of the heresy and support of the Bohemian heretics."[1] He himself confessed "that unfortunately I had not read Johannes Hus [yet] in Leipzig at the disputation."[2] The Hussites congratulated Luther for his disputation in Leipzig and sent him the pamphlet *De ecclesia* (*On the Church*) by Jan Hus (1369–1415).[3] Thus Luther read Hus, who had been burned as a heretic at the Council of Constance in 1415. He noticed his spiritual closeness to Hus and the Bohemian brethren who spread his teachings after his death at the

---

1 Luther's detailed report to Spalatin of July 20, 1519 (*LW* 31:321).

2 Martin Luther, *Von den neuen Eckischen Bullen und Lügen* (1529; *WA* 6:587.21–24).

3 Johann Poduška and Wenzel von Roždalowky to Martin Luther, July 17, 1519; Luther to Johann Staupitz, October 3, 1519 (*WA BR* 1:514.27–30).

stake,[4] saying that *De ecclesia* was a "highly understanding, noble, Christian booklet." Although Luther did not agree with many of the teachings, such as the seven sacraments, the celibacy of priests, and the vague position on the Lord's Supper, he provided only polite, friendly criticism and said, "It is true that I once called you heretics, while I was still a papist; but now I think differently."[5] Luther had thus fundamentally changed his view of the Bohemian brethren, and he maintained this view. As a result, relations with Wittenberg became ever closer. In 1520, just twenty-nine Bohemian students studied in Wittenberg, compared to eighty-eight ten years later.

Most important was the influence of Luther's Reformation on the reformulated Confession of the Brethren of 1535. This confession was also translated into Latin and handed over to later Emperor Ferdinand I, who had been their sovereign since 1526/27 as king of Bohemia. But Ferdinand's interest in the Bohemians and their faith does not seem to have been very intense. Luther was satisfied with the agreement reached regarding the Lord's Supper and baptism and was convinced that the differences that still existed could be endured in mutual Christian patience.[6]

Luther's praise spurred the Bohemians to continue working on this confession. It was ultimately reworked according to Luther's proposals and printed in Wittenberg. But the printing was delayed again and again, not because of Luther's disinterest, as the brethren suspected, but for financial reasons. Eventually the brethren themselves raised the necessary money, and Luther found a willing printer in Wittenberg in Georg Rhau (1488–1548), who took on the financial risk of printing. In 1538 the *Confessio fidei ac religionis baronum ac nobilium regni Bohemiae* (Confession of Faith and Religion of the

---

4 For the following, see Amedeo Molnár, "Luthers Beziehungen zu den Böhmischen Brüdern," in *Leben und Werk Martin Luthers von 1526 bis 1546*, ed. Helmar Junghans (Göttingen: Vandenhoeck & Ruprecht, 1983), 1:627–39.

5 Martin Luther, *The Adoration of the Sacrament of the Holy Body of Christ* (1523; *LW* 36:276).

6 Luther to Benedict Bavorinský, bishop of the Bohemian-Moravian Brethren, April 18, 1535 (*WA BR* 7:176 [no. 2189]).

Barons and the Nobility of the Kingdom of Bohemia) together with the reworked *Accountability of Faith* was published. The issues of penance and the celibacy of priests were also resolved in the direction of Luther's view. With regard to penance, the publication conceded to the faithful that they could make confession at the end of life, because God was gracious until death. The brethren did not want to recognize priestly celibacy as optional, as Luther would have preferred. However, they decided that if a priest could not keep celibate, he should tell the elders of the brethren, who would then accept this decision. As Czech theologian and historian Amedeo Molnár (1923–1990) explains, "Through the Wittenberg edition of the Latin version of the Confession of the Brethren, Luther manifestly recognized the Unity of Brethren as a member of the family of the churches of the Reformation."[7]

If we look at England, Luther's influence did not develop very positively there.[8] Already within a year of the publication of Luther's Ninety-Five Theses, his writings had reached England.[9] But King Henry VIII was still influenced by his lord chancellor, Cardinal Thomas Wolsey, who condemned this new movement in the strongest possible terms. The archbishop of Canterbury, William Warham, told Wolsey that Oxford University was "infected with the heresies of Luther."[10] It was also sad to see, he said, how especially the youth fell for these new teachings. Henry VIII then wrote a book against Luther on the seven sacraments (*Assertio septem sacramentorum adversus Martinum Lutherum*), which was presented to the pope, who in return conferred on Henry the title "Defender of the Faith" (*Fidei Defensor*). This publication was an attack on Luther, in which he denounced Luther as a heretic. Luther reacted in the same manner

---

7 Molnár, "Luthers Beziehungen zu den Böhmischen Brüdern," 637.

8 For the following, see James Atkinson, "Luthers Beziehungen zu England," in Junghans, *Leben und Werk Martin Luthers* 1:677–87.

9 Johann Froben to Martin Luther, February 14, 1519 (*WA BR* 1:332.26).

10 Letter no. 93, "Archbishop Warham to Cardinal Wolsey," in *Original Letters, Illustrative of English History*, ed. Henry Ellis, 3rd series (London: Richard Bentley, 1846), 1:239.

in *Against Henry the King of England* (*Contra Henricum Regem Angliae*), in which he attacked Henry VIII rudely and insultingly. These writings and other disputes increasingly alienated Luther and the king.

However, things changed when Henry VIII rejected his first wife, Catherine of Aragon, and married Anna Boleyn in 1533. As early as 1528, Pope Clement VII had secretly advised the king to simply marry Anna Boleyn and then see what to do. But when the pope once again emphasized the validity of Henry's first marriage to Catherine of Aragon, the king severed for himself and the English church the connection with Rome. In the Act of Supremacy of 1534, the king announced to his subjects that he was "the sole supreme head on earth of the Church of England" and the Parliament granted him the title of "Supreme Head of the Church of England."

Luther was asked for an opinion on the divorce between Henry and Catherine. But Luther, like the pope, thought that bigamy was preferable to divorce. This detailed and impartial advisory opinion, which was also shared by other theologians, was not to the king's liking, namely that the marriage should be maintained despite the difficulties. However, Henry continued to pursue the question of divorce, with English delegates negotiating with Wittenberg theologians. The matter was settled when Anna Boleyn was executed in 1536 on the king's orders.

When negotiations continued in Wittenberg, Luther was tired of them, because he thought they would only bring disagreements. He largely left these matters to his colleague Philipp Melanchthon. For King Henry VIII, political questions took precedence over theological ones. He sided with the Lutherans in the dissolution of the monasteries, since the dissolution meant huge financial revenues for the crown. On the issue of celibacy, however, he remained faithful to Rome, since there were no political or financial gains. Luther saw through these motives. Nevertheless, his Reformation insights had an impact in England, first through his writings and then later through consciously Protestant Christians who had studied in Wittenberg.

With regard to Scandinavia, Paul Helie was the authoritative theologian in Denmark.[11] He was a Carmelite provincial and lecturer at the University of Copenhagen with a humanistic tinge. However, when he read Luther's publication *On the Babylonian Captivity of the Church*, he turned away from Luther's theological approach. Nevertheless, he appreciated Luther as an important edifying writer, and in 1524 he translated into Danish Luther's *A Prayer Book, of the 10 Commandments, of the Faith, of the Lord's Prayer, and of the Hail Mary (Ein Betbüchlein, der 10 Gebote, des Glaubens, des Vaterunsers und des Ave Maria*, 1522). He became an important precursor of the Lutheran Reformation in that he distinguished between the actual Luther, who was heretical, and the points on which Luther was right and in accordance with the true Roman Catholic faith.

Particularly important for Luther's Reformation was King Christian II, who in 1520 forbade the publication of the bull in which Luther was threatened with church ban. In the same year he asked Elector Frederick the Wise to send him a preacher from Wittenberg. Influenced by humanistic ideas, the king wanted to modernize his university in Copenhagen and invited some scholars from Wittenberg to Denmark. However, in Denmark and Norway, which then belonged to Denmark, the nobility rose up against Christian II and forced him to flee in 1523. Soon after his deposition, Christian traveled with his wife to Wittenberg and visited Luther. Christian and his wife, Isabella, received Communion in both forms and thus professed the Lutheran faith. In Wittenberg they also made acquaintance with Melanchthon and Lucas Cranach, in whose house they probably lived until July 1524. Katherine von Bora, Luther's future wife, to whom Christian gave a golden ring, was also employed in this house. In 1524, the former king published the New Testament in Danish, the so-called *Christian II's Bible*. In the prefaces to the individual

---

11 For the following see Martin Schwarz, "Luthers Beziehungen zu Skandinavien," in Junghans, *Leben und Werk Martin Luthers* 1:689–97.

biblical books, polemics against the old faith are extremely strong and a case is made for the expelled king. Christian remained in correspondence with the Reformers throughout his life. In his writing *Whether Soldiers, too, Can Be Saved*, Luther presents the Danes who expelled Christian II as a negative example. Although Christian II was imprisoned until his death in 1559 for his futile coup to regain Denmark, he played a certain political role as the brother-in-law of Emperor Charles V, especially as he converted back to the Roman Catholic Church.

Christian's successor, King Frederick I, had to promise in 1523 that no heretic, a disciple of Luther, or anyone else would preach against God and the Roman Church. The Rigsrådet, a representation of nobility and clerics, banned Lutheran heresy in speaking and writing. Nevertheless, the king allowed Protestant preachers and prohibited the Danish bishops from seeking papal confirmation in the future. The Rigsrådet wanted at least a reformed Catholic Church under royal leadership. After King Frederick I married his daughter Dorothea to the Protestant Duke Albrecht of Prussia in 1527, Protestant schools of preaching were founded, and polemic literature directed against Catholicism was published.

When Christian III became king after Frederick's death in 1536, Protestant superintendents were appointed instead of Catholic bishops, and these superintendents were soon called bishops again. In 1537, the Reformation was officially introduced. Johannes Bugenhagen, who was the parish priest at St. Mary's in Wittenberg and also a disciple of Luther, crowned the royal couple and ordained the seven new superintendents, causing the church to lose apostolic succession. In addition, a new church order was issued and the University of Copenhagen was reopened, which had come to a standstill in the meantime. These three examples—England, Bohemia, and Denmark (which included at times also Norway and Sweden)—show the European influence of Martin Luther and his Reformation. Much more important, however, was the influence he exerted on other Reformers.

2. LUTHER'S INFLUENCE ON
REFORMED THEOLOGIANS

Luther's appearance at the Heidelberg Disputation in April 1518 left such a lasting impression on some Heidelberg humanists that their critical examination of tradition accelerated. Among Luther's enthusiastic supporters were leading figures of the later Reformation movement in southern Germany, such as Johannes Brenz in Schwäbisch Hall, Martin Bucer in Strasbourg, and Martin Frecht in Heidelberg and Tübingen. These theologians were also actively involved in the implementation and consolidation of the Reformation in southern Germany. However, one should not forget the indirect impact of Luther, namely, through the printing presses in Basel and Zurich through which Luther's Reformation ideas were widely disseminated.

The defenders and followers of the man from Wittenberg could not do enough to ensure the reprint of his writings, which also promised the enterprising printers a corresponding profit. This wide dissemination of Luther's writings, as well as the growth of his popularity after the Leipzig Disputation and above all his condemnation at Worms, meant that the term "Lutheran" served to describe the entire Reformation movement, especially from the opposing side. The word was synonymous with heretical or disbelieving.[12]

It is difficult to determine to what extent the reformer of Zurich, Huldreich Zwingli (1484–1531), was theologically influenced by Luther in his Reformation aspirations. The main point of contention between the two was the Lord's Supper: Were the body and blood of Jesus Christ really present in the Lord's Supper (real presence, according to Luther) or only spiritually present in the Lord's Supper, since Christ is actually at the right hand of God (according

---

12 Ulrich Gäbler, "Luthers Beziehungen zu den Schweizern und Oberdeutschen von 1526 bis 1530/1531," in Junghans, *Leben und Werk Martin Luthers* 1:482.

to Zwingli)? Landgrave Philip of Hesse invited the opponents to a religious discussion in order to eliminate the differences. As the final document of this Marburg Colloquy of 1529, Luther wrote the so-called fifteen Marburg Articles, to which the Swiss made some additions. From this it is clear that Luther agreed on fourteen points with Zwingli and the theologians influenced by Zwingli, such as Johannes Oekolampad (1482–1531) from Basel and Martin Bucer (1491–1551) from Strasbourg. The agreement included creation, the Trinity, Christ's redemptive work, infant baptism, and good works. Only in the longest and fifteenth article, concerning the Lord's Supper, could no complete agreement be reached.

It was agreed that the Lord's Supper takes place in both forms, that participation in the Lord's Supper is necessary for every Christian, and that the Lord's Supper moves the Christian to faith. However, it was not possible to agree on whether Christ was bodily present in bread and wine. Yet, a solution to the differing views was still hoped for: "And although at this time, we have not reached an agreement as to whether the true body and blood of Christ are bodily present in the bread and wine, nevertheless, each side should show Christian love to the other side insofar as conscience will permit, and both sides should diligently pray to Almighty God, that through his Spirit he might confirm us in the right understanding."[13] Luther had to accept that although he almost completely won over Southwestern German Protestantism, the Swiss Reformers finally decided against him.[14]

In addition to Zwingli, one should not forget another Reformed theologian, one from the second generation, so to speak, John Calvin (1509–1564), who was twenty-five years younger. Luther and Calvin never met in person, nor did they know each other's

---

13 *Marburg Colloquy and the Marburg Articles* (1529; LW 38:88–89), in the conclusion.

14 The break with Zwingli, one must admit, was also due to the crude and often personally hurtful manner in which Luther attacked Zwingli in the disputes over the Lord's Supper.

language. Luther could not speak French, and Calvin had access to Luther's German writings only through translations. Calvin sent a letter to Luther on January 21, 1545, but Melanchthon intercepted it, probably for fear that Luther would react unkindly. The letter contained two writings of Calvin on which he would have liked to have had an opinion from Luther. He had great respect for the Wittenberg Reformer and called him "the very excellent pastor of the Christian Church" and "my much respected father."[15] Calvin never lost respect for Luther, as shown in a letter to Heinrich Bullinger dated November 25, 1544, in which he writes of Luther's excessively passionate and daring character, with which he has serious faults but which is also rich in glorious virtues. Therefore, in his assessment, one must principally see Luther as "a most distinguished servant of Christ, to whom we are all of us largely indebted."[16] Conversely, there is only one direct statement by Luther about Calvin, in a letter to Martin Bucer dated October 14, 1539, in which he asks to extend greetings to Calvin, whose writings against Italian cardinal and humanist scholar Jacopo Sadoleto (1477–1547) he had read with great pleasure.[17] Similarly as with Zwingli, however, Luther notes that Calvin's understanding of the Lord's Supper is problematic. Luther mentions in a table talk, "Calvin is a learned man, but very suspicious of the error of the sacramentizers."[18] Luther realized that Calvin defended the Reformation doctrine with relentless seriousness, even if, according to Luther, he was not on the right track with regard to the doctrine of the Lord's Supper.

Finally, we want to take a look at Eastern Europe.

---

15 Letter 124, John Calvin to Martin Luther, January 21, 1545, in *Letters of John Calvin*, compiled by Jules Bonnet (Philadelphia: Presbyterian Board of Publications, 1858), 440.

16 Letter 122, John Calvin to Heinrich Bullinger, November 25, 1544, in *Letters of John Calvin*, 433–34.

17 Martin Luther to Martin Bucer (*LW* 50:191 [no. 287]).

18 Martin Luther, table talk 6050 (1531–1546; *WA TR* 5:461.18–19).

3. LUTHER'S INFLUENCE IN EASTERN EUROPE

Luther's influence was also felt in Eastern Europe.[19] In 1518, indulgence preacher Johann Tetzel wrote in a letter to papal nuncio Karl von Miltitz, "The Augustinian Martin Luther has turned the powerful against me not only in all German lands, but also in the kingdoms of Bohemia, Hungary and Poland in such a way that I am not safe anywhere."[20] Probably as early as 1518, prints and pamphlets from Wittenberg came to Eastern Europe through merchants and students. Since Luther's Ninety-Five Theses were printed in German translation soon after their publication in Nuremberg, German-speaking citizens in Hungary and Transylvania were able to quickly get to know Luther's criticism of the church. Although Archbishop Georg Szakmári, then the primate of Hungary, ordered that Luther's teaching be condemned from all pulpits in the country, there were already determined followers of Luther among the priests and university teachers. Even the strict measures adopted by the Hungarian Diet in 1523 and 1524 against all Lutherans and their patrons could not eradicate the deep sympathy for Luther. Students from various southeastern European countries were already enrolled at Wittenberg University at that time and contributed much to the spread of the Reformation in their home countries. Between 1522 and 1600, 1,018 students from Hungary alone studied in Wittenberg. I was told at the Reformed University in Debrecen that every student who studied in Wittenberg was to bring home one book, which then was added to the university library.

Many Christian warriors and dignitaries, including King Ludwig II of Hungary and Bohemia, were killed in the Battle of Mohács against Ottoman ruler Suleiman I in 1526. In the ensuing political and economic confusion, many longed for a consolation, which they found in the Lutheran Reformation. At the time of Luther's death, more than half of the population of Hungary and Bohemia

---

19 For the following, see Tibor Fabriny, "Luthers Beziehungen zu Ungarn und Siebenbürgen," in Junghans, *Leben und Werk Martin Luthers* 1:641–46.
20 Quoted from Tibor Fabriny, "Luthers Beziehungen zu Ungarn," 641.

was sympathetic to the Lutheran faith. Since Luther had heard that
Mary, the wife of Ludwig II, had sympathies for Luther's teachings,
after the disaster of Mohács he sent her in December 1526 *Four
Comforting Psalms to the Queen of Hungary* (*Vier tröstliche Psalmen
an die Königin von Ungarn*). Formally, the queen always remained
faithful to Rome. Nevertheless, in September 1531, Luther wrote her
a letter in which he comforted her that everything could go away
on earth "if only the grace remains with us that God is our Father,
his Son our brother, his heaven and creature are our inheritance,
and all angels and saints are our brothers, cousins and sisters."[21]
The significant influence of Luther is also reflected in that Thomas
Stoltzer (ca. 1480–1526), the court musician of Queen Mary, set to
music various psalms that were translated into German by Luther,
and composed and performed a motet on Psalm 37. The congregations in Hungary had adopted eleven of Luther's hymns by 1569, and
through his influence the first hymnals with notes were published
in Hungary.

Luther also served as a theological counselor. Thus, Count Franz I
Reway from today's western Slovakia turned to Luther because of his
Zwinglian doubts about the real presence of Christ. The Reformer
responded to the Hungarian count in a letter dated August 4, 1538,
by encouraging him to stand firm in the right doctrine of the Lord's
Supper.[22] The count then sent a theology student to Wittenberg, who
was enrolled there in 1538. Important also was Leonhard Stöckel,
praeceptor Hungariae (the teacher of Hungary), who had studied in
Wittenberg with Luther and Melanchthon. He introduced in Upper
Hungary a new school order characterized by humanistic educational
methods. The two reformers of central and Upper Hungary, Matthias
Dévay (ca. 1500–1546) and Leonhard Stöckel (1510–1560), remained
in close contact their entire life with Wittenberg, where they had

---

21 Martin Luther to the queen of Hungary (1531; *WA BR* 6:196.25–30 [no.
1866]).

22 Martin Luther to Count Franz von Reway, August 4, 1538 (*WA BR*
8:258–61 [no. 3246], esp. 260.22–25).

studied together in 1530. Through Luther's correspondence with persons in this region, it is evident that he was particularly interested in the ecclesiastical and theological development of Hungary, including today's Slovakia and Transylvania.

Luther's position as the initiator of a worldwide Reformation was due on the one hand to his immense literary production and on the other hand to the invention of modern letter printing with movable type, through which a text could be assembled from individual letters into words, sentences, and entire pages, since about 1450. Due to the simultaneous invention of the printing press, it was then much easier to reproduce the individual pages than if they were laboriously copied by hand. To Luther's surprise, his Ninety-Five Theses of 1517 spread throughout Germany in no time at all, "as if the angels themselves had been messenger runners," as Friedrich Myconius, a contemporary of Luther, wrote.[23] Luther's *Sermon of Indulgences and Grace* from 1518 appeared in more than twenty editions with a total of more than twenty thousand copies, a hitherto unheard-of book success. In addition, he regularly preached in the city church St. Mary's and also in the castle church. Decisive for his broad impact, however, was his professorship at the University of Wittenberg. He helped the faculty of theology to rise to first-class importance within the university. In the founding year of the university, a total of 416 students were enrolled there, while in 1520, 579 enrollments were already recorded.

Until 1540, annual enrollments averaged 221. In 1544, with 814 students, the highest number of enrolments in the 16th century was achieved. In the decade between 1535 and 1545, more than 4,700 enrolments took place. Wittenberg had the most students in these years compared to the other German universities. They came from numerous European countries, especially Scandinavia and Southeastern Europe.[24]

---

23 Friedrich Myconius, *Geschichte der Reformation*, ed. Otto Clemens (Leipzig: Voigtländer, 1914), 22.

24 Heiner Lück, "Wittenberg, Universität," in *Theologische Realenzyklopädie* 36:234.

Even after Luther's death, Wittenberg enjoyed high enrollment figures. They ranged between four hundred and eight hundred annually. Since Luther taught at the university until the end of his life in 1546, he shaped many future theologians, who carried his teachings to all the countries of Europe.

QUESTIONS FOR DISCUSSION

How did Luther view the problem of King Henry's VIII's divorce? How did his view compare to the pope's?

What was Luther's view of the Lord's Supper, and how did it differ from Zwingli's?

Luther's reformation succeeded in no small part due to the printing press. How do today's technologies influence the spread of religious messages?

CHAPTER THREE

"By Grace Alone": A Unique Feature of the Lutherans?

Often the contrast between Protestant and Catholic is seen in that Catholics can acquire eternal bliss through good works, whereas Protestants have only to believe in Christ, since good works do not contribute toward salvation. This opinion is further substantiated by the fact that most Roman Catholic churches are magnificently decorated, whereas Protestant places of worship sometimes seem downright barren.

Of course, the Reformation was sparked by the sale of indulgences, when Luther noticed that the faithful were buying letters of indulgence thinking that with their monetary payments they would be relieved of the punishments in purgatory without having to repent their sinful lives. Luther, on the other hand, claims in thesis 7 of his Ninety-Five Theses of 1517, "God remits guilt to no one unless at the same time he humbles him in all things and makes him submissive to this vicar, the priest."[1] The remission of a guilt requires a humble attitude, which entails a corresponding change of heart. We cannot bargain with God as we would with a human being, because God is God. We can only humbly ask God for forgiveness, vow

---

1 Martin Luther, Ninety-Five Theses (1517; *LW* 31:26).

improvement, and hope for pardon. Reformed Swiss theologian Karl Barth (1886–1968) therefore speaks of "the 'infinite qualitative distinction' between time and eternity," since God is in heaven and we are on earth.[2]

But how can we bridge this distance and come to God? For many people in the Middle Ages, it was clear that only good works would help to make God gracious. As a child of his time, this was also the opinion of Luther when the question, "How do I obtain a gracious God?" drove him to the monastery. In Luther's time, life expectancy was very short. When he died at not even sixty-three years old, his body was weakened by disease, and he was an old and frail person. Life at that time was full of hardship and suffering. People were helpless in the face of diseases such as plague, kidney stones, or high blood pressure, to name just a few. Comforts that we take for granted today were hardly available at the time, such as glass windows or heated living spaces. When Luther traveled from Wittenberg to Rome, he did so on foot and was on the road for several weeks.

1. HOW DO I OBTAIN A GRACIOUS GOD?

Since one could expect little from life on earth, one wanted at least to make sure that there was a gracious God who granted one a pleasant life in the hereafter. Therefore, everything possible was done to make God gracious. The faithful went on pilgrimages, made large donations to the church, acquired relics of well-known saints, joined a monastery (like Luther did), or bought letters of indulgence so that the time one spent in purgatory would be made as short as possible. It was no coincidence that Luther joined the Augustinian hermits. They were known as a strict order, and Luther thought that if he led a strict monastic life, his chances would be better that God would be gracious to him at his life's end. Therefore, he took the requirements

---

2 Karl Barth, *The Epistle to the Romans*, trans. from the 6th ed. by Edwyn C. Hoskyns (London: Oxford University Press, 1968), 10.

of the monastery very seriously. If, for example, he missed one of the prescribed services, he made up for it later. He once confessed, "If a monk ever went to heaven because of his monastic life, I wanted to have gone in."[3]

But Luther did not find inner peace through his pious activities. On the contrary, he felt more and more that God would not accept him, because he could never live as God asked him to. Eventually, Luther realized that there is nothing people can do on their own to make God gracious. No prayers, no good works, no services or pilgrimages, or whatever humans could come up with would be enough to make God gracious. God is God and does not allow himself to be influenced by us. As a good Augustinian, he recognized, like Augustine, that the "free will is sufficient for evil, but is too little for good, unless it is aided by Omnipotent Good."[4] When we forsake God, we are forsaken and cannot return to God on our own. There is no way from us to God. No matter how high we jump, we always fall back to earth.

We can illustrate this with an example that is certainly true for many people: imagine we did not take God seriously for years because career, family, and earthly pursuits were more important than God. God should not interfere in our lives. But in old age we think more about the end of life. We become more pious and turn to God. If we were to assume that God is happy about such a conversion, that God is finally taken seriously, we have a completely inadequate idea of God. In fact, Jesus said that God rejoices over one sinner who repents. But Jesus said nothing about God being happy when we use God as we please. First, we push God into the corner so that he doesn't get in our way. But then we turn to God so that God may grant us eternal life. No, God is God. God is not the senile old man in heaven who is happy that someone finally wants to use him again. No, God does not need us. He is truly God.

---

3 Martin Luther, *Kleine Antwort auf Herzog Georgen nächstes Buch* (1533; WA 38:143.26–27).

4 Augustine, *On Rebuke and Grace* 31, in *NPNF*[1] 5:484.

In his famous writing *On the Bondage of Will* (1525) Luther emphasizes that we cannot turn to God or the devil on our own. It is the other way around: God and the devil are fighting over us. That is why we are either ridden by the devil or guided by God. What should we do, then, if our power is insufficient to turn to one of them? Are we just puppets who have to do what God or Satan has in mind for us? The answer of most people, in Luther's time or even today, would probably be, "Not quite." Although God is sovereign and almighty, God will not ignore us when we live a pious life or do good works. Luther, however, realized that this calculation did not work. He did not get a clean conscience despite all his efforts, because God does not reward us for something we should do anyway, which is to live a pious life and do good works.

Luther thus realized that the righteousness that counts before God does not come from our efforts but is attributed to us by God. We are never righteous, that is, sinless, before God. But God is not the merciless judge Luther knew from the medieval piety in which he grew up. God is a gracious God. But how do we know that God is gracious and merciful? Isn't that just human imagination, a fancy idea that everything will come out all right? The realization that God is God and is therefore so superior to us that we can never reach God by ourselves, but only God can bridge the gap between Godself and us—this knowledge can also be found in other religions. As Luther drastically puts it, even the devil could arrive at such an idea. What matters, however, is not how God is in general but how God relates to each and every one of us. How can we find this out? Luther refers here to Jesus, the human face of God. He argues that "the incarnation of Christ powerfully calls us away from speculating about the divinity," because God "came into the flesh, presenting the flesh to us, in which we might behold God dwelling bodily." Christ alone "is our way to God."[5] In the historical Jesus of Nazareth, God made himself tangible and showed us his heart.

5 Martin Luther, *Lecture on Isaiah* (1527–1629; LW 16:55), on Isa 4:6.

2. IN CHRIST, GOD HAS MADE
GODSELF COMPREHENSIBLE

In Jesus, the finite and the infinite came together. Through God's action, the infinite qualitative difference between us and God has been bridged. Just as Luther writes in his Christmas carol "From Heaven Above":[6]

> These are the signs which you will see
> To let you know that it is he:
> In manger-bed in swaddling clothes
> the child who all the earth upholds.

In the child Jesus, the Creator and Sustainer of the whole world came to us.

In another verse of the same song, Luther writes:

> This is the Christ, God's Son most high,
> who hears your sad and bitter cry;
> who will himself your Savior be
> and from all sin will set you free.

Christ is our Savior. He can deliver us from the bondage of sin and open the gate of heaven to us. He can do this because he is the human face of God and the one in whom God shows us God's heart. According to Luther, this is the great difference between the Christian faith and all other religions and philosophies. These have respectable insights into what God is like in general, but only in Jesus Christ do we have the specific knowledge of how God is toward us. Through Jesus, we see that God is gracious God and invites us to trust him, and that God spares nothing to save us from finitude and human self-deception.

---

6 Martin Luther, "From Heaven Above," in *Evangelical Lutheran Worship*, hymn 268, stanzas 5 and 3.

The cross of Christ is the hermeneutical key to God's salvation history and especially to the Christ event. Luther claims that no one could have invented a cross as the means of salvation. If we humans had come up with a sign of our salvation, we would have chosen something great and wonderful, but not an ignominious cross. However, the cross shows God's characteristic way of creation out of nothingness. God saves in a way that no one thought possible, not even Jesus's closest circle of disciples. Everyone thought that with Jesus's death everything was over. But then came the decisive turning point, the resurrection of Jesus by God. Since this cannot have been invented, it reflects the history and actions of God for our salvation. That is why Luther assures, "Only the cross is our theology."[7] And, "True theology is practical, and its foundation is Christ, whose death is appropriated to us through faith."[8] By practical theology, Luther means an existential theology as opposed to speculative or theoretical theology. This practical aspect becomes immediately clear in Luther's explanation of the second article of the Apostles' Creed in his *Small Catechism*. After the confession of the true Godhead and true humanity of Jesus Christ, this twofold nature is at once explained in its immediate effects for salvation. Salvation is accomplished through the innocent suffering and death of Christ. This was done for us.

The emphasis of the cross is not a negative theology, or a theology of the absurd, that Jesus, for example, had to suffer and die as the human face of God. On the contrary, the cross is realistic because it shows the characteristic way of God's working. No one would assume that something good could arise if someone died on the cross abandoned by all his friends. But it is precisely this sign of defeat that God chose as the starting point for the victory of life. In his greatest compassion, God turned this sign of defeat around and made it a sign of victory over death and the starting point for a new creation.

---

7 Martin Luther, *Operationes in Psalmos* (1519–1521; WA 5:176.32–33), on Ps 5:12.

8 Luther, table talk no. 153 (1531/32; LW 54:22).

God is the one who brings about salvation in and through Christ without our intervention. We hear nothing here about the participation of the saints or Mary, because as Luther said, "She is the servant because she has born to me God's son so that I can believe in him."[9]

But how do I know that God shows me his heart in Jesus? Are there not many other embodiments of the deity or avatars? Luther knew nothing of the numerous Hindu gods or the many human embodiments of these gods, but he knew the cult of saints and of Mary of his time. He appreciated the saints, especially Mary, because they can serve us as a model for a godly life and thus have an educational function. But they have no mediating function between us and God, and, according to Luther, they cannot contribute anything to our salvation. The reason for this is simple: God chose to show Godself to us only in Jesus Christ and not in one of the saints.

Only through the human nature of Jesus can we draw nearer to God, for "the humanity is that holy ladder of ours . . . by which we ascend to the knowledge of God."[10] Through the impression of Jesus's proclamation and destiny we realize that God loves us. Through him we get a proper understanding of God and God's work. Jesus is not important because he was such a good preacher, because he worked miracles, or because of his holy life. He is crucial for us because he is the mediator of God's redemptive activity. With this emphasis on God's redemptive activity in Christ, all other ways in which Christians in the Middle Ages wanted to reach God, to understand God's will, or attempted to turn God favorably to them were recognized as useless. Christ alone was Luther's decisive insight.

As we said, the reason for "Christ alone" lies in God's decision to only reveal Godself in Jesus. Luther also recognized that this divine self-disclosure depended on the unique relationship between God and Christ. To fully convey God, Jesus could not just be a saint or an avatar. He must be completely and wholly God. Otherwise he would not have been able to mediate God. At the same time, Christ had to

9 Martin Luther, *Predigt über Johannes 1:1–3* (1522; WA 11:227.12–13).
10 Martin Luther, *Lectures on Hebrews* (1517/18; LW 29:111), on Heb 1:2.

be completely and wholly a human being. Otherwise he would not have been able to reach us and identify with us. In being one with the Father, which Luther affirmed with the Council of Nicaea, Christ was able to convey God. That is why Luther emphasizes, "Christ does not consist of soul and body, but of humanity and divinity. He has not only assumed human nature, meaning that he consists of body and soul."[11] Then he states, "What Christ suffered can also be attributed to God, for they are one."[12]

Although Luther paid careful attention to the tradition of the church, especially the church fathers, he did not trust in human words. He emphasized that he would not follow the writings of Augustine or any other theologian unless the Bible confirmed them. He even says, "One can rather believe a simple layperson quoting the Bible than the pope or a council that does not quote the Bible."[13] Our knowledge of Christ must not be based on theological deductions or human conclusions if it is to be credible, but only on God's word, as attested by the Bible. Scripture alone is the ultimate foundation of our faith. By emphasizing the Bible as the only source of our knowledge of salvation, does Luther not introduce the Bible as a paper pope instead of the pope in Rome? Luther would vehemently disagree with this assumption, because what is written in the Bible is not correct because it is just in the Bible.

Luther was not a biblical literalist, and unlike John Calvin, he did not exegete one biblical book after another. For Luther there were central writings and passages in the Bible and peripheral writings. Central to him was everything that clearly communicated Christ. Everything else that has almost nothing to do with Christ, such as, for example, large parts of the Jewish ceremonial law or the Epistle of James, are marginal writings. Luther criticizes: the Epistle of James

---

11 Martin Luther, *Disputation de divinitate et humanitate Christi* (1540; WA 39/II:110.22–23).

12 Luther, *Disputation de divinitate et humanitate Christi* (WA 39/II:121.1–2).

13 Martin Luther, *Contra Malignum I. Eccii judicium M. Lutheri defensio* (1519; WA 2:649.2–3).

"wants to teach Christians, and does not even commemorate in such long doctrine the passion, the resurrection, the Spirit of Christ. He mentions Christ several times, but he teaches nothing of him, but speaks of a general faith in God."[14] For Luther, faith did not mean that certain things were true, such as the pronouncements of the church councils or the pope, or every letter of the Bible. For him, faith was personal trust, trust in Jesus Christ, who communicated himself to us through the Bible and leads us to the Father, who alone can give us salvation in the hereafter and guidance in our present life. This means that Luther leads back to the central doctrine of the Christian faith—God in Christ, both sovereign and merciful, who accepts us without any preconditions and to whom we respond with a faith active in love.

In the Second Vatican Council the Roman Catholic Church did not arrive at the insight "Scripture alone" when it stated, "There exists a close connection and communication between sacred tradition and Sacred Scripture. For both of them, flowing from the same divine wellspring, in a certain way merge into a unity and tend toward the same end."[15] But at the same time, with a quote from the Church Father Jerome, the Catholic Church emphasizes that "ignorance of the Scriptures is ignorance of Christ." If we want to understand Christ correctly, then, in the spirit of Luther, the Roman Catholic Church refers us to the Bible. But what about good works?

3. THE FUNCTION OF GOOD WORKS

Decisive things have also happened recently with regard to the theology of good works. For Lutherans, October 31 is considered a

---

14 Martin Luther, *Preface to the Epistle of St. James and Judae* (1522; WA DB 7:384.19–22).

15 *Dogmatic Constitution Dei verbum: Revelation* 2.9, 6.25, in Heinrich Denzinger, *Compendium of Creeds, Definitions, and Declarations on Matters of Faith and Morals*, 43rd ed., ed. Peter Hünermann (San Francisco: Ignatius Press, 2012), 922, 929.

day of remembrance of the Reformation, because on this day in 1517 Martin Luther posted his Ninety-Five Theses on the door of the Castle Church in Wittenberg, the bulletin board of Wittenberg University. On that very day in 1999 Cardinal Edward Idris Cassidy, the president of the Pontifical Council for Promoting Christian Unity, and Christian Krause, the president of the Lutheran World Federation, signed in the Evangelical Lutheran Church St. Anna in Augsburg the "Historical Joint Declaration on the Doctrine of Justification." The Methodists joined the declaration on July 23, 2006, with the signatures of President Bishop Sunday Mbang and General Secretary George Freeman. On July 4, 2017, at a ceremony held in St. Mary's Church in Wittenberg, the World Communion of Reformed Churches joined the declaration, which was signed by Secretary-General Chris Ferguson. A little later the Anglicans also joined this agreement. This joint declaration expresses basic agreement on God's justification of Christians "by grace alone."

In the preamble the declaration says:

> We confess together that all persons depend completely on the saving grace of God for their salvation. The freedom they possess in relation to persons and the things of this world is no freedom in relation to salvation, for as sinners they stand under God's judgment and are incapable of turning by themselves to God to seek deliverance, of meriting their justification before God, or of attaining salvation by their own abilities. Justification takes place solely by God's grace.[16]

Here it is stated that in this central concern of Luther the Lutherans and the Catholics are of one mind, namely that by grace alone humans are accepted by God, that is, they are justified before God. At the same time, it is stated that the mutual doctrinal condemnations from the sixteenth century no longer apply regarding what the other side taught on the justification of the sinner before God. In the Reformation period, the unity of the Western church was broken by the dispute over justification and the practice of indulgences. With the joint declaration and the additional documents, the churches that

---

16 "Declaration on the Doctrine of Justification," 19.

had been separated since the Reformation succeeded for the first time in making joint statements on the doctrine that was once the starting point for the division. The doctrinal condemnations relating to the doctrine of justification have thus lost their church-dividing effect.

Of course, even with this agreement, there were theologians for whom the texts went too far or, conversely, did not go far enough. Already a year before the signing, 160 German Protestant theologians opposed the joint declaration. Concerns were raised that the Lutheran position was not clearly enough enunciated. On the other hand, the Congregation for the Doctrine of the Faith, chaired by its prefect, Cardinal Ratzinger, pointed out that there were still divergent positions between the two denominations. It was also doubted that the Lutheran World Federation was really a partner with binding authority, since it did not have jurisdictional power like the Roman pope.

Despite these criticisms, it should not be overlooked that an important building block for the unity of the churches was laid here, even if there were no immediate ecumenical consequences. The mutual doctrinal condemnations of the sixteenth century, which were repeatedly quoted against the other side, were finally declared outdated. This removed an important stumbling block. In addition, it was recognized that one can really only come to God by God's grace. Cardinal Gerhard Ludwig Müller, the successor of Cardinal Ratzinger as prefect of the Congregation for the Doctrine of the Faith, confessed in an interview in 2017 that Martin Luther had been right in his criticism of the sale of indulgences. The sale of indulgences was a "fraud against the faithful."[17] Instead of excommunicating Luther, the Catholic Church should have distinguished more critically what he actually wanted. For Luther, grace alone was at the heart of our relationship with God. Through the joint declaration, the Roman Catholic Church also committed itself to this. However, when Pope John Paul II proclaimed a holy year the following year,

---

17 Cardinal Gerhard Ludwig Müller, interview, News Service of the Roman Catholic Church in Germany, April 11, 2017.

which was associated with an indulgence, the unique characteristic of the Christian faith, "by grace alone," was relativized again.

But are good works completely superfluous for Luther? Can we simply sit back, so to speak, and let God be a good guy, for God will make things come out all right? With such a sentiment Luther would be completely misunderstood. He emphasizes very clearly, "Good works do not make a good man, but a good man does good works."[18] As a matter of fact, many and great good works are done by a pious person. Luther writes: "Good works do not make good, just as the fruits do not make a good tree, but a good tree brings good fruit, and a good man creates a good work. A good man and a good tree grow without works by faith in the truth of God's Word alone."[19] Luther is concerned here with the right order: First comes God, and then come we humans. God accepts us by grace, and in our response to this, we are also gracious to others, that is, we do good works. If we do not do this, then we have not understood what God has done for us without any preconditions. In medieval understanding, God always played a major role with the grace he showed us, but the good works were, so to speak, an assurance that God would really show us mercy. But Luther remarks that if we have to contribute even a small part to our bliss, then bliss will be on shaky ground. God will certainly do his part, because God is reliable, but what about us? That is the reason Luther emphasizes grace alone, because God keeps what God promises. But with us it is uncertain.

Good works are therefore by no means superfluous; they are even necessary, but not as a precondition of salvation but rather as a consequence of the joy of the salvation we have received. It was always important to Luther that our good works benefit the people who need our help and not simply God. So he says in a sermon, "Also called are these not good works that we do to God; but which we are to do to our neighbors, these are good works."[20] These works, of course,

18 Martin Luther, *The Freedom of a Christian* (1520; LW 31:361).

19 Martin Luther, *Resolutio disputationis de fide infusa et acquisita* (1520; WA 6:95.15–18).

20 Martin Luther, sermon, April 27, 1522 (*WA* 10/III:98.15–17).

are not done without God, for Luther remembers Jesus saying to his listeners, "Just as you did it to one of the least of these who are members of my family, you did it to me" (Matt 25:40). That is why Luther writes, "Every work of a Christian man should be a service to God."[21] For Luther, everything we do is ultimately a service to God, though it is done for our fellow human beings. As Luther explains, all our actions are simultaneous worship: "The service of God is not bound to one or two works, nor is it expressed in one or two estates, but is distributed into all works and estates."[22]

Good works or social commitment on this earth are not a precondition for our salvation. They would be completely inadequate. However, they are our natural reaction once we realize we are undeservedly accepted by God. God has made us, who had been alienated from him, into Christians without any preconditions. Since God is good to me, I will also be good to others. Since God was merciful to me, I will also be merciful to others. The ethical behavior of Christians is thus a reactive behavior. It is motivated by the realization that God loves us unconditionally. However, Luther was also a realist and admitted that we are very good at asking but not at giving thanks. Therefore, the grace alone of Lutherans, but not only of them, was often misunderstood as a carte blanche for inaction toward God and humans.

QUESTIONS FOR DISCUSSION

For Luther, how does a sinner become a saint?
What does it mean that the cross is the "hermeneutical key" to salvation history?
What is the theological significance of the *Joint Declaration on the Doctrine of Justification*?

---

21 Martin Luther, *Predigten aus den Jahren ca. 1514–1520* (Lenten sermon; WA 4:653.1).

22 Martin Luther, *Christmas Postil 1522* (Luke 2:33–49, Gospel on the Sunday after Christmas; *LW* 75:416).

CHAPTER FOUR

God Is Unfathomable

Until the beginning of modern times, it was self-evident for most people to believe in God, for nature and human reason testified to the existence and work of God. The situation changed with the Enlightenment of the seventeenth and eighteenth centuries and the flourishing of scientific-technical knowledge of the world and its domestication in the nineteenth and early twentieth centuries. Philosopher Immanuel Kant (1724–1804) took note of this new situation and wrote in the preface to the second edition of his *Critique of Pure Reason* against the British empiricists, "I therefore had to annul knowledge in order to make room for *faith*."[1] At the same time, he refuted the proofs of God that had hitherto been accepted as valid and showed that we cannot prove anything beyond that which we find in the world. God and God's works cannot be fathomed with our reason. Charles Darwin (1809–1882) later agreed with this sentiment when, on the one hand, he discovered strict rules according to which all living beings evolved, and on the other hand, he did not consider it possible that all this could happen without God's doing. For more and more people, however, it was clear that God had become "unemployed."

This is drastically demonstrated with the following anecdote. When French mathematician and astronomer Pierre Simon Laplace

---

1 Immanuel Kant, *Critique of Pure Reason*, unified ed., trans. Werner S. Pluhar (Indianapolis: Hackett, 1996), 31 (B xxx).

(1749–1827) presented Napoleon a copy of his five-volume *Celestial Mechanics*, the emperor curiously asked him what place God occupied in his system. Laplace is said to have proudly replied, "Sire, I did not need this hypothesis." As God had become unemployed in our world, more and more theologians avoided associating God with nature. God was, so to speak, imprisoned in the ghetto of the human soul. Dietrich Bonhoeffer writes that we must live in the world as if God did not exist. "Our coming of age leads us to the true recognition of our situation before God. God would have us know that we must live as men who manage our lives without him."[2] However, Bonhoeffer's conclusion that we are moving toward a nonreligious world was wrong. It is true that the number of those who break away from the church, whether Protestants or Catholics, is constantly increasing, so that the large churches in Europe and North America will soon become minority churches. But this does not mean that more and more people are becoming nonreligious. This may be true for the citizens of the so-called new federal states in Germany and for the Czech Republic, but the vast majority of people have some faith—in a higher being, in a higher power, or even in angels, who are becoming more and more popular. Since today an increasing number of people cherish their independence in every respect, they do not want to be told by a certain denomination what to believe. They put together their own religion, borrowing from Buddhism, Christianity, and pagan ideas.

Luther would have agreed with the understanding of such a patchwork religion, because he was convinced that all people have a faith, that is, are religious, even those who are not Christians. He explains what he means in his interpretation of the first commandment in his *Large Catechism*:

> A "god" is the term for that to which are to look for all good and in which we are to find refuge in all need. Therefore, to have a god is

---

2 Dietrich Bonhoeffer, *Letters and Papers from Prison*, rev. and enlarged ed., ed. Eberhard Bethge, trans. Reginald Fuller (New York: Macmillan, 1967), 188.

nothing else than to trust and believe in that one with your whole heart. As I have often said, it is the trust and faith of the heart alone that make both God and an idol. If your faith and trust are right, then your God is the true one. Conversely, where your trust is false and wrong, there you do not have the true God. For these two belong together, faith and God. Anything on which your heart relies and depends, I say, that is really your God.[3]

All humans have something they rely on and have their heart attached to it. This serves them as god, be it their intellect, the career, or family. But from this general awareness of something ultimate there is no direct path to the knowledge of who God really is. Luther fluctuates in his assessment of this natural knowledge of God, because on the one hand he criticizes it as a projection of our own desires and our reason, but on the other hand he regards it as an actual knowledge of God. The reason is that he asserts a twofold knowledge of God: a general one that is present in all people in some way, and a special one that is conveyed through Christ alone. He writes, "There is a twofold knowledge of God: the general and the particular" (*Duplex est cognitio Dei, generalis et propria*).[4] The general or natural knowledge of God, as we have seen above, is first of all based on Luther's broad understanding of who or what God is.

1. NATURAL KNOWLEDGE OF GOD
FROM GOD'S WORKS

In a sermon Luther addresses the ambiguity of the natural knowledge of God:

The whole world names as God that in which humans put their trust in times of distress and trial, that in which they take comfort and depend upon, and that from which one desires to receive all good things and

---

3 Luther, *Large Catechism*, 386.
4 Martin Luther, *Lecture on Galatians* (1535; LW 26:399).

that can provide help. This is what the pagans have done when they first of all made Jupiter a helper and a god. . . . Afterwards they created many false gods based on their reason. The Romans established any number of gods which were necessary to help them with their various activities, so that one helped people in war, one was given this power and another that power; one was to make corn to grow, another to help at sea in case of shipwreck. As many needs, good things, and uses as there were upon earth, so many gods were chosen until they also made plants and garlic into gods. . . . This way does reason describe God: He is that which helps a person, is useful, and beneficial. One detects here that reason only knows as much about God as Paul attributes to it in Romans 1:19–21 when he says that one knows that God is.[5]

Because God has inscribed this knowledge indelibly in the human heart, it cannot arise from human reason. Epicureans and other atheists indeed sought to deny this awareness of God, "but they do it by force and want to quench this light in their hearts. They are like people who purposely stop their ears or pinch their eyes shut to close out sound and sight. However, they do not succeed in this; their conscience tells them otherwise."[6] We could even say today that human beings are innately religious, since everybody senses that there is something beyond us, whatever we might call it. Hence Luther rightly emphasizes in his exposition of Jonah, "Such a light and such a perception is innate in the hearts of all men; and this cannot be subdued or extinguished."[7] Pagans, for instance, called on their gods, whom they really believed to possess a divine nature. "This demonstrates that there was in their hearts a knowledge of a divine sovereign being." All religions testify to the existence of a divine being who is invisible, eternal, and powerful. Therefore, human beings are naturally aware of the ultimate contingency and dependence of their existence. We are neither responsible for our own

---

5 Martin Luther, *Predigten über das 5. Buch Mose* (1529; WA 28:609.29–610.19), on Deut 5:6.

6 Martin Luther, *Lectures on Jonah* (1526; LW 19:54), on Jonah 1:5. The Epicureans, named after the Greek philosopher Epicurus (ca. 341–ca. 270 BC), were known for their fearlessness before the gods and their pursuit of happiness.

7 Luther, *Lectures on Jonah* (LW 19:53), on Jonah 1:5.

existence, nor do we fully control it. "Because of a natural instinct the heathen also have this understanding; they know that there is a supreme deity."[8] Luther makes frequent reference to Romans 1:19-21 when here and elsewhere he contends that "they have a natural knowledge of God."[9] Natural perception of God and general knowledge about God did not originate from human beings, for nature, as God's creation, already testifies "that humans shall call upon God."[10] In order to rightly honor God, Jews received the law from God at Mount Sinai, while gentiles were given the law in their hearts. No one is excluded from the natural knowledge of God, for "there has never been a nation so wicked that it did not establish and maintain some sort of worship."[11] In light of the universal veneration of God, Luther always stresses that all people "have the general knowledge, namely, that God is, that He has created heaven and earth, that He is just, that He punishes the wicked, etc."[12]

By what means do people obtain this the natural knowledge? Here we encounter first the law, then reason, and finally philosophy.

Knowledge of God through Natural Law

According to Luther, the knowledge of God that is gained from the ethically obligatory law, for example the Ten Commandments, is a common possession of all people. "Reason is familiar with the knowledge of God which is based on the law," explains Luther.[13]

> For to have a God is not alone a Mosaic law, but also a natural law, as St. Paul says (Rom. 1:20), that the heathen know of the deity, that there is a God. This is also evidenced by the fact that they have set up gods

---

8 Martin Luther, *Commentary on the Epistle to the Romans*, trans. J. T. Mueller (Grand Rapids: Kregel, 1976), 43, commenting on Rom 1:19.

9 Martin Luther, *Lectures on Genesis* (1535–1545; *LW* 3:117), on Gen 17:7.

10 Martin Luther, *Über das 1. Buch Mose. Predigten* (1527; *WA* 24:9.20–21).

11 Luther, *Large Catechism*, 388, on the first commandment.

12 Martin Luther, *Lectures on Galatians* (*LW* 26:399), on Gal 4:8–9.

13 Martin Luther, *Sermons on the Gospel of St. John* (1517/38; *LW* 22:150), on John 1:18.

and arranged forms of divine service, which would have been impossible if they had neither known nor thought about God. For God has shown it to them.[14]

Hence the Ten Commandments, according to Luther, belong to the category of general or natural knowledge of God, and indeed blend together with natural knowledge in many ways. Natural law, which is found in its purest form in the Ten Commandments, demands the honoring of God in the first table (commandments 1–3) and requires the love of one's neighbor in the second table (4–10). Since God has engraved the natural law equally into the hearts of all people, we are able to know God. In the twentieth century, comparative ethology has discovered that Decalogue-like prescriptions are present in many cultures and even in the animal kingdom. These prescriptions further social contacts and survival in general.[15]

Knowledge of God through Reason

Luther was very skeptical of the use of reason and of philosophical reflection. He knew that humans could quickly find a "reasonable" argument that allowed them to do what they wished to do and to avoid doing what God wanted. Likewise, he held philosophy to be too speculative, for it produced many claims about God that Luther thought clearly contradicted Scripture. These limitations notwithstanding, he viewed reason and philosophy as originally being good gifts from God through which people were able to know much about God. Especially in *On the Bondage of the Will* (1525), Luther stresses that reason is able to say some things about God, for there is no reason that does not recognize God. This reasoned knowledge of God is gained from God's work, particularly creation, and from God's rule,

---

14 Martin Luther, *Against the Heavenly Prophets in the Matter of Images and Sacraments* (1525; *LW* 40:96–97).

15 See Ernest Thompson Seton, *The Ten Commandments in the Animal World* (Garden City, NY: Doubleday, 1925), and Wolfgang Wickler, *The Biology of the Ten Commandments*, trans. D. Smith (New York: McGraw-Hill, 1972).

that is to say, from the divine working in history. This knowledge did not originate with human beings but God, who gave us reason in order that we might know God.

"God has planted such light and understanding in human nature so as to give us an indication and a picture of his divine rule and shows us that he alone is Lord and creator of all creatures."[16] Reason, for example, opens up the possibility of ascertaining a Creator and Sustainer on the basis of teleology and order in nature in the so-called proofs of the existence of God. Even the knowledge of God from those laws recognized by humans can be categorized epistemologically under reason, for reason understands God's commandments and with it the distinction between right and wrong. Nevertheless, our knowledge of God based on reason does not stand on firm ground because, as Luther well knew, people do not want to believe that God punishes sin, and therefore they prefer to follow their own thinking. They tend to compromise this knowledge and speculate about God through their own rational reflections. Natural reason can indeed know "that this Godhead is something superior to all other things," so that all people can call on a divinity.[17] Yet this God-given knowledge is often perverted through human high-handedness and leads to idolatry, that is, to the following of other gods rather than the true God.

Knowledge of God through Philosophy

Philosophy, which Luther uses almost interchangeably with reason, also turns its attention to the created order and deduces from it who rules the world. It knows that there is a first mover (*primum movens*) and a highest being (*summum ens*), as Plato (428/27 BC–348/47 BC) already showed. Yet the will of the Creator remains hidden from reason, for humans are blinded by their sinful self-centeredness

---

16 Martin Luther, "Epistel am Sonntag Trinitatis. Röm 11:33–36," *Crucigers Sommerpostille* (1537; WA 21:510.39–511.1).

17 Luther, *Lectures on Jonah* (*LW* 19:53), on Jonah 1:5.

and cannot see the world as it really is. Of course, the Platonists concluded in their speculations that God is spirit, rules the world, and is the ground of all that is good in the natural order. But they were so blinded by the sovereignty and majesty of God in his works that in their search for God they did not recognize God. Why God made things the way God did and why God rules in the way God does are questions for which philosophers have no answers.

The speculative knowledge of God produced by philosophy also fails in the end because it focuses on the naked majesty of God (*nuda majestas dei*), which is beyond human comprehension. According to Luther, speculative philosophy seeks to reach the beyond from the here and now. As Kant later demonstrated, this is impossible because God cannot be reached from a human starting point. Luther admits that speculative philosophy is able to discern some things about God. Yet it often becomes lost in abstract speculation.

Intuitive Knowledge of God through God's Works

To this point we have seen that for Luther God cannot be fathomed by our senses. At the same time, Luther firmly believed that God could be intuitively known by us. He explains in one of his table talks:

> One cannot comprehend God, yet one senses his presence, for he lets himself be seen and known by one and all and he reveals himself as a good creator who acts for our good and gives us all good things. This is attested by the sun and moon, heaven and earth, and all the fruits which grow from the earth. But the fault does not lie with the creator that in such works and in his innumerable good acts we do not recognize God, as if he desired that he should be hidden from our eyes. No, the fault lies not with God but with us, for human nature is so corrupted and poisoned through original sin that we are not able to notice, let alone know and understand God.[18]

It is not God's fault but our own that the experiential and intuitive knowledge of God from his works is so ambiguous. Human

---

18 Martin Luther, "Tischrede," table talk 6530 (undated; *WA TR* 6:20.19–29).

beings want to comprehend God from a human starting point and from the natural order. But because of our sinful turning away from God, we are no longer able to clearly perceive God. Nevertheless, the natural order allows us to perceive something of God. Nature reflects something of the deity, for it teaches "that there is a God, who gives us all things good and helps us against all evil."[19] This intuitive sensing of God's working in nature and history is one of the roots of human religiosity and of the worship of God in the world religions. Luther agreed with the tradition of the Middle Ages that one could detect the footprints of God in nature. But to what extent is this a true knowledge of God?

Speculative reason can reach the conclusion that God can do all things. But this fact does not yet tell us anything about the direction and intention of God's activity. Through reason we can determine the attributes of God: God is almighty, eternal, all-knowing, and so on. But we cannot thereby know God's will. The recognition of the power and greatness of God is a fundamental moment of all religion, for it is written in the heart of every person that God is all-powerful and all-knowing. Further, we are able to recognize that God is just. We do not worship God as an impersonal highest being, but rather seek to enter into a dialogue with God that involves calling on him and receiving something from him. "Therefore, all men know that God is our Refuge, and they implore his help and protection."[20] In the hearts of all people is implanted the knowledge that God helps and upholds those in distress and in crisis. Nevertheless, this God-given knowledge, according to Luther, has been wrongly interpreted, for these deeds are not attributed to the true God but rather to false objects, namely, idols. People can indeed be monotheists, that is, believe rightly that there is but one God, but this, too, can be twisted into the worship of a false god. The knowledge that there is a deity who is just, helps in time of need, and guides and rules all things

---

19 Martin Luther, *Eine kurze Form der zehn Gebote, des Glaubens und des Vaterunsers* (1520; WA 7:205.17).

20 Luther, *Lectures on Genesis* (*LW* 7:336), on Gen 43:23.

is not accorded to the one God but is transferred to a pseudo-god or an idol.

According to Luther, we encounter here a threefold limitation of general knowledge of God. First, without the self-disclosure of God in Jesus Christ the knowledge of God is subjective, for it lacks the corrective of the revelatory Christ event. Second, knowledge of God is threatened by the sinful efforts of human beings to change the true knowledge of God through their own wishes or conceptions. Finally, general knowledge of God is only a preliminary stage on our way to God, in view of his revelation in Jesus Christ, which as a better alternative replaces general knowledge. Those who continue to follow a general knowledge search for a God of their own wishes and desires, and not the true God, who discloses Godself finally in Jesus Christ. Luther says in his lecture on Deuteronomy, "Where there is no Word of God, there is no true knowledge of God; where there is no knowledge of God, there are godless ignorance, imaginations, and opinions about the true God."[21]

The Subjectivity of General Knowledge of God

According to Luther, the most severe problem of the natural knowledge of God is its subjective character. Because everyone pictures God as they see fit, the result is diverse human forms of God's veneration, because "as each one shapes a god for himself, so he also worships."[22]

Similarly, natural law, which is supposed to be binding for our ethical behavior, is interpreted in different and often contradicting ways. Some consider good what others despise as bad and vice versa, for the orders established by God can be understood in conflicting ways. In Luther's view, God always encounters us just as we imagine God to be. If we think, for example, that God is angry, then God is so for us. "The God you believe in is the God that you have. If you believe that God is gracious and merciful, you will have such

---

21 Martin Luther, *Lectures on Deuteronomy* (1523/24; *LW* 9:53), on Deut 4:3.
22 Luther, *Lectures on Jonah*, Latin text (1525; *LW* 19:11), on Jonah 1:4.

a God."[23] General knowledge of God, therefore, adapts itself to our own subjective conceptions, so that God becomes that in which we trust and what makes us happy. With this result we are confronted with a subjective projection of God. That does not mean, however, that God adapts to suit our wishes; it means only that our conceptions of God are changeable. Instead of trusting in God, we believe in a deity of our own wishful thinking. Hence it is, according to Luther, of utmost importance to have "a correct and proper feeling about God."[24]

That we believe in God is not decisive, but rather that we believe rightly in God, or, what for Luther was the same thing, that we believe in the true God. The danger of projection in a general knowledge of God consists in that this knowledge is not guided by God but is adapted to our own wishes. For Luther, an example of this is found in pagans, who "did not worship this divinity untouched [that is, the deity as manifested to them] but changed and adjusted it to their desires and needs."[25] Because general knowledge of God has no corrective outside the created order, it usually proclaims a projection of human desires as God.

The Limits of General Knowledge of God

As Luther continually emphasized, all of us have some inkling of God. But we usually develop it in such a way that it results in a caricature of God. Our sense and understanding transform our knowledge about God into a fantasized picture. The idolatry that follows from this is a distortion of the true religion and led Luther to comment sarcastically that "religion, however, is the greatest of all human achievements."[26] Since autonomous human reason does not

---

23 Martin Luther, sermon, September 10, 1525 (WA 17/I:412.19–20), on Luke 17:11–13.

24 Luther, Lectures on Jonah, Latin text (LW 19:11), on Jonah 1:4.

25 Luther, Lectures on Romans (LW 25:157), on Rom 1:19.

26 Martin Luther, Vorlesung über Jesaia (1527–1529; WA 25:383.10–11), on Isa 65:1.

permit to be guided by God, its understanding of God is wrong and inappropriate. Thereby religion deteriorates to a pseudo-religion, and the veneration of God becomes the veneration of other gods. Luther would even agree with the thesis of an original monotheism, that all people originally pursued one religion. But then this religion was fragmented and deteriorated to different rival religions. We can only speak of a true knowledge of God in today's religions in terms of basic general convictions of a supreme being, but not in concrete details.

Due to our alienation from God, we cannot correctly interpret God's activity in the world. We tend to confuse cause and effect and to see ourselves as the author of that which is actually God's work, while at the same time we view our own work as coming from God. The work of God, however, should not be difficult to recognize, for it always aims at the preservation and salvation of both us and the world. Since God uses the cooperation of his creatures as his instruments in sustaining and working in the world, humans are often led to the false assumption that they themselves are the agents of this work. Also, in observing the natural order, humans often conclude that everything takes place by natural means and that nature is grounded in itself. The sinful alienation of human beings from God has already progressed so far that they dispute the efficacy of God and put the causes of all occurrences down to immanent effects. God, in the process, becomes superfluous. Because the natural knowledge of God is prone to so many misunderstandings, it cannot serve as the starting point of faith for Luther.

2. SPECIAL KNOWLEDGE OF GOD
THROUGH GOD'S SELF-DISCLOSURE

According to Luther, there is only one appropriate knowledge of God, namely, God's Word, which took on human form in Jesus Christ. Hence Luther writes that, just like Christ, God is everywhere present: "He does not desire that you wander all over looking for him, but where the Word is, there you should go; and then you grasp him correctly. Otherwise you tempt God and fall prey to idolatry. For this reason, God has given us a particular manner as to how and where we would seek and find God, namely through the Word."²⁷ Luther rejects the natural knowledge of God for Christians when he says, "It is extremely dumb to want to know God. Therefore, one should remain with the Word" (*Stultissimum, ut darnach trachten eum cogoscere. Idea haerendum in verbo*).²⁸ Seen from the perspective of Christian faith, the natural knowledge of God is able to tell us very little. "If God had wished to be known to us through reason, then God would not have come to us in the flesh."²⁹ Through the revelation in Christ, the knowledge of God has taken on a new and deeper dimension because, as Luther writes in his exposition of Jonah, a great advantage is to be seen is this manner of revelation: "So there is a vast difference between knowing that there is a God and knowing who or what God is. Nature knows the former—it is inscribed in everybody's heart; the latter is taught only by the Holy Spirit."³⁰

The knowledge of God through the revelatory Christ event takes place through God alone. God becomes human and thereby is able to be known by us, yet as the object of our knowledge God remains always God. God manifests God's self to us in his self-disclosure in a concrete human form. For Luther, revelation in this context implies first of all the self-manifestation and self-objectification of God. The logical epistemological premise that something can only be known by that which is similar to it remains valid here. Hence God takes the initiative in the act of revelation and in its acknowledgment. Revelation is not a lesson about God that relates to us certain facts about God, but rather a self-disclosure in which God makes his own self known. God discloses himself either in human hearts or in an external word. According to Luther, revelation in the human heart is not a mystical indwelling of God but is comparable to the

27 Martin Luther, *Sermon von dem Sakrament* (1526; WA 19:492.22–26).

28 Luther, *Predigten über das 5. Buch Mose* (WA 28:608.8–9).

29 Martin Luther, *Vorlesungen über Jesaia* (1527–1529; WA 25:106.43–44), in a scholium of 1534 on Isa 4.

30 Luther, *Lectures on Jonah* (LW 19:55), on Jonah 1:5.

knowledge that God has taken on human form. God does not, however, reveal God's self in such a way that God is fully absorbed into this revelation, for despite becoming human, "God does not leave heaven."[31] This self-disclosure not only tells us that God is and what God's attributes are but discloses to us God's internal and otherwise unfathomable being. Hence, in contrast to the general knowledge of God, this knowledge does not remain a surface knowledge but leads to God's innermost intentions.

In God's self-disclosure that which is without limits takes on a bodily form—the person of Jesus Christ. God is not comprehensible unless God allows his own self to be comprehended. In analogy to the real presence of Christ in the Eucharist, in which the living Christ is present in bread and wine, the omnipresent God becomes visible to us in the revelatory Christ event in a specific place and time. That which is finite is enabled to take up the infinite into itself. Humans find God, therefore, in visible form in the historical revelation of the Christ event. When God discloses God's self, God must at the same time enter into the created order, into the categories of space and time, to encounter us beneath the mere outward appearance of that work.

Incarnation as God's Entry Point into History

The almighty, infinite God came in the incarnation of Jesus Christ into our finite world. For this reason, Luther calls the incarnation God's greatest work, which contradicts all the rules of human logic. The life of Jesus is the center point of God's self-disclosure, for in a unique, historical event in the fate of a concrete, historical person, the Eternal One entered into history. The place we can comprehend God is not in nature, as pantheism claims, but in the life of a single, historical person. The humanity of Jesus becomes our point of access to the unfathomable transcendence of God. God becomes knowable

---

31 Luther, *Predigten über das erste Buch Mose* (1523–1524; WA 14:213.13), in sermon on Gen 11.

for us by entering into creation in space and time, that is, in the categories in which God works in the natural order and in which we are able to know God. As Luther writes in his Christmas hymn "From Heaven Above":

> These are the signs which you will see
> to let you know that it is he:
> in manger-bed, in swaddling clothes
> the child who all the world upholds.[32]

When God becomes a part of human history, God also comes into contact with our sinful alienation from him. Yet God does not become sinful but instead deals with our sin. Jesus Christ, as the wholly Other, stands completely on our side in order to bring God to us. God's order has been distorted through the antigodly powers of destruction, but Christ lives within it so that through him God can come close enough to us that we are able to recognize God. Because God takes on human form in his self-disclosure, anthropomorphic characteristics of this revelation are unavoidable.

Anthropomorphic Characteristics of God's Self-Disclosure

God has not changed in this self-disclosure. As accommodation to our finite nature, which is alienated from God and which the infinite God cannot accept, God has disclosed his own self in the incarnation in a way that is appropriate to human beings. Since God came to us in a human being, we make use of anthropomorphic concepts to describe God's activity. For instance, we say that God speaks to us in a friendly manner, is happy, sad, or suffers, metaphors that can be seen especially in the Old Testament, which Luther interprets in a Christocentric manner. We must necessarily speak of God's works using human concepts or else remain silent. This does not mean that God becomes a new being in this self-disclosure, but rather that God

---

32 Luther, "From Heaven Above," stanza 5.

shows to us what God really is and always has been in a hidden, transcendent being.

But this self-disclosure is not a depiction of God in which God still remains secluded. God does not exhaust his own self in this self-revelation but still remains in his almighty sole activity an enigmatic God, the hidden God (*deus absconditus*) who makes us tremble. But over against this unfathomable God, who causes many people to shake their heads or even to anxiety and despair, Luther distinguishes the revealed God (*deus revelatus*), who desires our communion with him in Jesus Christ. The distinction between God as he is (*deus ipse*), who according to Luther is not our business, and the revealed God guards Luther against a radical personification of the idea of God. This would then have meant that God is nothing other than a fully perfected human being, something philosopher Ludwig Feuerbach (1804–1872) contended.

God cannot be fully grasped in the personal categories we use to describe him. God is not a person who has eyes, ears, and vocal cords, but God always assumes personal traits if God discloses himself. We cannot make any concrete statements about the very being of God, God's very self, but only about the word of God. God is revealed and manifests his loving will in God's word and in his Son. What God is like in and of God's own self is neither of interest to us nor necessary for our salvation. Only God's self-disclosure, God's word, and the gospel are decisive for us. These deductions show that Luther had no interest in a speculative theology but only in a theology spawned by the practical life issues of human beings. He once explained in a lecture, "The true knowledge [of God] does not consist in speculation but moves forward to action."[33] If we have realized who God is, a gracious and caring God, then for us Christians there are consequences in works of thankfulness. All understanding of God results from God's self-disclosure in Jesus Christ and has immediate practical consequences for our lives.

---

33 Martin Luther, *Lectures on the First Epistle of St. John* (1527; LW 30:238), on 1 John 2:3.

Knowledge of God through Christ

In a table talk from 1531–1532 Luther declared, "True theology is practical, and its foundation is Christ, whose death is appropriated through faith" (*Vera theologia est practica, et fundamentum eius est Christus, cuius mors fide apprehenditur*).[34] Three aspects of this statement are important:

1. The foundation of theology is Christ.
2. The work of Christ is only understood only through faith.
3. True theology is practically oriented, that is, it is directed toward the redemption of human beings.

Luther, in an anti-speculative way, centers his theology in Christ and the redemption he has wrought. Only through the person of Jesus can one rightly draw near to God, for "the humanity [of Christ] is that holy ladder of ours . . . by which we ascend to the knowledge of God."[35] The unique position of Jesus consists in that it is through the imprint of his words and actions that we come to the knowledge that God loves us. Jesus is the loving connection and the comforting glimpse to God. Only when we begin with Christ are we able to make appropriate statements about God and God's work, because through the unity of the will of Father and Son, God relates to us just as the Son relates to us. In Jesus Christ, the human face of God, God has disclosed to us his heart. True knowledge of God is not speculation about God but rather the knowledge of the Father's will, which is made known in the sending of the Son.

Luther can even make the extreme claim that "the visible God was fully hidden to humanity before the advent of Christ."[36] It is only through Christ that we are able to move from an outside view of God to an inside view. From the actions of God in Christ we learn that God loves and accepts his creation. Christ, therefore, is not

---

34 Luther, table talk 153 (*LW* 54:22).

35 Luther, *Lectures on Hebrews* (*LW* 29:111), on Heb 1:2.

36 Martin Luther, *Dictata super Psalterium* (1513–1516; *WA* 3:143.9–10), on Ps 25.

primarily significant as preacher, miracle worker, or moral teacher, but as mediator of the redemptive divine will. Christ points to the goal of God's work, which moves unalterably toward its completion, toward the triumph of God's loving will in a new, purified creation. Yet in Luther's view it is not sufficient to simply look to Christ, because others do that as well and then interpret him according to their own preferences. We must rather look correctly to Christ.

The Theology of the Cross as Guiding Principle

As we have already noticed, Luther contends, "The cross alone is our theology" (*CRUX sola est nostra Theologia*).[37] He separated himself thereby from a mystical or speculative theology and centered all his thinking on the revelation of God in Christ. The cross of Christ becomes the center from which one must view all theological statements. In adopting this approach, Luther does not follow the popular medieval theology of the imitation of Christ but stresses instead the nearly incomprehensible outrageousness of the Christ event, because this Christ suffered in our place. The theology of the cross, which focuses on the historical figure of Jesus and his death on the cross, stands in contrast to every speculative theology that consciously and in light of concrete human history seeks to make understandable God's saving activity. Luther never tires of emphasizing that Jesus and his death on the cross contradict all human ideas about what God must do to achieve our salvation. Hence, we dare not begin with how God (according to our own ideas) must act, but we must instead hold firm in our thinking to how he actually did act.

3. THE THEOLOGY OF THE CROSS AS TRUE THEOLOGY

Reformed theologian Jürgen Moltmann (b. 1926) states in the vein of Luther, "*Theologia crucis* is not a single chapter in theology, but the

---

37 Martin Luther, *Operationes in Psalmos* (1519–1521; WA 5:176.32–33), on Ps 5:12.

key signature for all Christian theology."[38] This was indeed Luther's conviction, because the theology of the cross enables us to understand the incarnation of God. Hence Luther emphasizes in the *Heidelberg Disputation* of 1518 that "true theology and recognition of God are in the crucified Christ" (*Ergo in Christ crucifixo est vera Theologia et cognitio Dei*).[39] If we want to know God, then we must not attempt to force our way directly to the majesty of God through reason but must rather focus on the incarnation of God. The sign under which God's self-disclosure in Christ must be seen is the cross, for this is the work of God that destroys and condemns our "reasonable" deliberations. If we would have thought out God's salvation, we would have thought of something great and impressive and not of a shameful cross. Therefore, salvation on the cross cannot be a human invention.

God wills to be known in the weakness of the crucified Christ so that he might annihilate our wisdom, which imagines God's revelation to be very different. The cross as the sign of God's self-disclosure also guards against deceitful imitations. While the majesty of God can easily be counterfeited into a fantasized image of our own ideas, the cross will not be imitated or distorted by any religion, philosophical speculation, or our own fantasy. The cross cannot be a human invention. Humans would have never thought that God would let his Son die on the cross in order that we might be redeemed. Apart from this, the cross of Christ also means that Christ, as a sign of his solidarity with humans, intentionally wishes to be weak in order to place himself on the same level as humans and to suffer along with us on earth.

For Luther it is an outrageous thing that God would be born as a child and die on a cross. One cannot understand this event through human speculation. Instead, God must lead our understanding if we are to recognize the meaning of this event. Whoever bypasses

---

38 Jürgen Moltmann, *The Crucified God: The Cross of Christ as the Foundation and Criticism of Christian Theology*, trans. R. A. Wilson and John Bowden (Minneapolis: Fortress, 1993), 72.

39 Martin Luther, explanation of thesis 20 of the *Heidelberg Disputation* (*LW* 31:53).

Christ does not recognize God hidden in him. Such persons are called "enemies of the cross" by Luther because they discard the value system of God. They label as bad the good of the cross, that is, the incarnation of God; and they call good all that is bad in their own thoughts, that is, their abstract, philosophical reasoning.[40] Although the cross looks bad and unappealing on the outside, it is not something bad but rather something good, because Christ and thereby God has made it his own and has destroyed the bad works of the exalted. Bad works are those through which we hope to succeed before God, including speculative theology, through which we attempt to fathom God by our own power.

The theology of the cross, however, not only points to the cross as the humbling and becoming human of God; it is also for Luther an indication that God always works under the appearance of the opposite. With the Christ event it became evident for Luther that God brings to perfection when he destroys, that God makes alive when he crucifies, that God saves when he sits in judgment, indeed, that God reveals himself when he conceals himself. Hence Luther can name the cross the true negative theology.[41] God works, according to Luther, like a dental surgeon who makes dangerous, difficult, and disfiguring incisions but nevertheless does good work.[42] Even if one is at first afraid that things are only going to get worse, nonetheless the surprising healing process comes in the end, and the pain is replaced by a feeling of well-being.

Two aspects of this work of God under the appearance of the opposite need special emphasis:

1. Every self-achieved knowledge of God shatters on the cross of Christ. Luther once said that there is no religion which according to reason seems so absurd and stupid as the Christian religion, yet he nevertheless believes in Jesus Christ. Through the hiddenness of God in his saving work on the cross, all the wisdom of the world

---

40 Luther, explanation of thesis 21 of the *Heidelberg Disputation*.
41 See Martin Luther, *Selected Psalms II* (1534–1535; *LW* 13:111), on Ps 90:7.
42 Luther, explanation of thesis 6 of the *Heidelberg Disputation* (*LW* 31:45).

is refuted. God wishes to be recognized only in suffering and to condemn all wisdom that seeks to comprehend the invisible things with the help of visible things. God must open our eyes so that we can rightly recognize his miraculous work, the cross of Christ, and its true meaning.

2. An ascending knowledge of God that seeks to work its way up from us to God, or one that, in contrast, begins with the mysteries of God, is destined to fail. God can only be known when we allow ourselves to be guided by God to God's astounding work on the cross.

Why does Luther so strongly emphasize the hiddenness of God's work under the appearance of the opposite? He intends thereby not just to say that God does not wish to be sought where God has not disclosed Godself; it is also decisive for Luther that God alone, in the revelatory event, is the only one who is active. God chose the way of the cross that he might remain the sovereign Lord of all saving work and of the entire revelatory event. No one expected this event to occur as it actually did. Even the so-called astrologers inquired first in Jerusalem about the newborn king of the Jews, not in unimportant Bethlehem (Matt 2:2). God and God's self-disclosure cannot be comprehended by any rational principle. Only on the basis of that which has taken place can we describe it, and then only in approximation. Even then we depend on God's help in interpreting this event.

Central for Luther's understanding of the Christian faith is the Godhead of God. Since there is this unbridgeable dimensional difference between us and God, there is no cooperation possible between us and God concerning issues pertaining to salvation. The first step always comes from God, to which we then can react appropriately. This first step of God is a totally unexpected gift. Just like with the creation at the beginning, there appears life for us out of nothingness, from the death of Jesus. At the same time and under the appearance of the opposite, the death of Jesus becomes his victory and our salvation.

Luther rejects any kind of atheism by rightly claiming that everyone has some kind of God to which one's heart clings. In so doing he affirms the possibility of a knowledge of God in terms of a general revelation caused by God. In principle such revelation is accessible through reason. As we can detect from the multitude of religious viewpoints, this general revelation is ambiguous. Clarity, according to Luther, is only possible through God's self-disclosure, in which God makes Godself visible in the human form of Jesus of Nazareth. Through Jesus's conduct and destiny, we are able to recognize God in an unmistakable way. Therefore, Jesus is the yardstick for the proper knowledge of God amid the plethora of religious ideas, and at the same time the ladder to God.

QUESTIONS FOR DISCUSSION

Why did Luther view speculative knowledge of God with suspicion?
How does Jesus "disclose" God?
Why is the "theology of the cross" important for all theology?

CHAPTER FIVE

The Gospel Is Not a Law

The strict distinction in the biblical message between law and gospel seems to be a typically Lutheran idiosyncrasy. For instance, Reformed theologian Karl Barth writes, "As the doctrine of God's command, ethics interprets the law as the form of the gospel."[1] Here the distinction between law and gospel is overcome, and the law is, so to speak, subsumed under the gospel. Yet the danger of a new legalism arises, as one often encounters in Calvinist and pietistic communities. Though the liberating power of the gospel is emphasized, one hears for the most part the demands of the biblical message, so that the law, so to speak, becomes the other side of the gospel. Especially in evangelical circles but also in contemporary Protestantism, the gospel is used in the legalistic, or rather moralistic, way to demand from Christians a Christlike conduct. Many secular people also live under the law. They live under the relentless demands that society exerts on them or to which they subject themselves so that they can meet the prevailing norms and expectations of society. They live and work continuously under the threat of the law. The liberating message of the gospel has been superseded by the law.

---

1 Karl Barth, *Church Dogmatics*, vol. 2, *The Doctrine of God*, part 2, ed. G. W. Bromiley and T. F. Torrance (Edinburgh: T&T Clark, 1957), 509.

Luther, however, insisted on a strict distinction between law and gospel whereby both should neither be mixed nor separated. He had gotten to know of the disadvantages of the late Middle Ages ethos of obligation and compensation, first in popular piety and then as a monk. Therefore, he emphasized that in the gospel God frees us from all legal obligations. This freedom should never be changed to a new legalism. Instead, the one word of God must always encounter us in the twofold perspective of law and gospel.

1. ANTITHESIS AND UNITY OF LAW AND GOSPEL

God's law has always been known to humans because it is inscribed by nature in our hearts since creation. Luther teaches this in agreement with Paul. Even if humans never had the written law by Moses, they would know by nature that they must honor God and love their neighbor. The spirit of God, Luther says, dictates the law into the hearts of all people. But God's will, which is expressed in the law and which enlivens and enlightens human reason, is misunderstood since the fall through the sinful desires of humanity. Therefore, God has given the people of Israel through Moses a written law, which should remind the people of the natural law in their hearts. According to Luther, Moses is not the author of the Mosaic law, but he interprets the natural law in the Mosaic law most clearly.

According to Luther, one must consider the law in a twofold way. It is the summary of the eternal will of God, and as such it condemns the sinner. Thereby one must distinguish between the content of God's law and its expression in which it confronts this sinner. According to its content, it is the eternal will of God, and its fulfillment serves our salvation. For instance, we should not infringe on or offend the Godhead of God. If we conduct ourselves according to God's will, God will be gracious to us. The law as God's eternal will has always been in force. Even in the world to come it will still be present, but as completely fulfilled. Therewith the law has an original, a present, and a future significance. It is the eternal and unchangeable will of God. Yet with the fall, the relationship changed fundamentally between the law, meaning God's eternal will, and us humans. God's eternal will became for us as sinners, who live distant from God and in opposition to God, the law with which God confronts us. The content stayed the same, but the shape of the law had changed. This we need to see now in more detail.

The term *law* contains a double meaning, a civil or worldly one and a theological or spiritual one. From the worldly side its task is to fend off the big transgressions and crimes in a world that is characterized by sin and also to maintain public peace. In this world the law is effective through the estates introduced by God, that is, worldly authorities, parents and teachers, and secular laws. In this secular form humans can fulfill God's law and obtain civil justice. We can live within the framework of these secular laws without breaking them. From this secular or civil use, a second perspective or use of the law must be distinguished, which Luther calls the "true" use. We encounter this use, for instance, in the Sermon on the Mount, when Jesus tells us that we should always live in unity with God and God's will. Through this radical exposition of the law, God's will is intensified in the extreme. From us a pure heart and complete obedience to God is expected.

The law understood in this way could have been met prior to the fall, when humans were living in union with God in the garden. But for us sinful people, the law is impossible to meet. The law no longer helps us to be righteous before God, since we cannot fulfill it. To the contrary, the law reveals our sinfulness and even increases it. From the knowledge that we cannot fulfill the law comes hatred against God and despair, as Luther himself admitted when, as a monk in the monastery, he failed to lead a life in harmony with God. God appears to be unfair because he demands more than we can do. Therefore, the law continuously accuses us and hands us over to the wrath of God, to judgment, and to eternal death. This was Luther's devastating insight.

All people know something about this accusing law of God, but they have no real knowledge of God's mighty will since they have not felt it. They live according to the motto, "I am not perfect, but God will forgive me because he is a loving God." The law must be announced to such people that they are brought out of this slumber and attain the true knowledge of God and of God's will. Then they feel the power of the law and are called to repentance. The original love of God by which the law should lead them to a God-pleasing life has now become a tool of God's wrath. This theological aspect of the law shows humans how far they have actually moved away from God.

If one wants to pronounce just the gospel and omit the law because it frightens people with God's wrath, one refuses to be confronted with the truth about God. Luther therefore turns against the antinomians, that is, those who rejected the theological aspect of the law and wanted to ban it from the church. They claimed, "The Decalogue belongs in the town hall, not in the pulpit." Luther refers here to Paul (Rom 4:15) and argues that if there is no law, we do not recognize that we sin and transgress against God's will, that is, the law. "It follows that if there is no sin (since the Law has been abolished), there is also no Christ as Redeemer from sin."[2] Only through our sinful life, which is uncovered through the law, almost like holding a mirror to our face, do we understand who we are and why Christ had to die for us. Moreover, for Luther the law is necessary for salvation because without the law humans stay distant from God, since they do not realize how far they have removed themselves from God. Through confrontation with the wrath of God and the recognition of our own failures, we are driven to God and to his gospel. Next to the law there is the gospel, the other side of God's word.

Law and gospel have entirely different, even opposing, functions. The law establishes what we should do and what we are not allowed to do, and as a consequence of human failure, it accuses and condemns us. The gospel, on the other hand, has as its content God's promise that Christ died for us and sacrificed himself for us. It proclaims

---

2 See Martin Luther, *Antinomian Theses Circulated among the Brethren* (1537; *LW* 73:48), where the claim of the antinomians is cited, which he attacks in the subsequent theses; *LW* 73:55.

that all the demands of the law have already been fulfilled in Christ. Therefore, thanks to Christ, our sins, which separate us from God, are forgiven. Luther then writes in his commentary to Paul's Letter to the Galatians of "the preaching of the remission of sins through the name of Christ, that is, the Gospel."[3] With Paul, from whom Luther took over the characterization of the gospel as promise, Luther contrasts law and gospel. The gospel as good news announces the grace of God that for the sake of Christ, God no longer counts our past failures against us. As Christians we can begin a new life. The law leads to death, but the gospel gives eternal life through the liberation provided by Christ. The law places us under the wrath of God; the gospel, however, brings grace. Law and gospel stand contrary to each other in that through the gospel the justification of the sinner occurs, contrary to what is possible through the law. It is the liberating gospel that must be believed, not the law that demands our condemnation. Justification takes place, as Paul says, *apart* from the law. Luther goes a step further than Paul at this point and says *against* the law.[4]

Law and gospel, however, are related to each other, even in their opposition. Law and gospel must indeed be clearly distinguished from each other, but they cannot be separated, just as they also cannot be blended together. When they are separated from each other and only the law is announced, there ensues a new legalism according to the motto, "A Christian is not allowed to do this or that." If only the gospel is announced, there results, as Dietrich Bonhoeffer calls it, "cheap grace," as he explains, "Cheap grace means the justification of sin without the justification of the sinner."[5] We shy away from naming that which traditionally was called sin as sin because we do not want to offend anybody. This postmodern mentality creates new insecurities because there are no longer any binding rules with regard to right and wrong. If law and gospel are blended together, then there

---

3 Luther, *Lectures on Galatians* (*LW* 27:184), on Gal 1:12.
4 See Martin Luther, *Die Promotionsdisputation von Palladius und Tile-mann* (1537; *WA* 39/I:219.23–24), thesis 36.
5 Dietrich Bonhoeffer, *The Cost of Discipleship*, rev. and unabridged ed., trans. R. H. Fuller (New York: Macmillan, 1979), 46.

ensues, as previously mentioned, a legalistic morality, which follows prevailing trends because there, too, the binding character is limited by whatever is in.

For Luther, however, law and gospel are inexorably connected. The gospel presupposes the law and its unfolding because only when we know the demands of the law and the will of God can our sins be forgiven. If it were otherwise, the pardoning of sins would not make sense, because allegedly we have no sins. Sin can only be recognized if one knows the law. Therefore Luther, in his dispute with the antinomians, could say, "If the Law is removed, sin is also removed, and if sin is removed, Christ is removed, as there would be no use for Him."[6] The good news of Christ's saving work and the redemption from sin can be neither understood nor desired if one has not recognized the extent of human estrangement from God, as seen from the vantage point of the law. The gospel needs the law, for it is the preaching of the law that is the indispensable and necessary presupposition of preaching the gospel. Without the law as a criterion of God's will, humans cannot realistically judge their own abilities but remain self-confident and even arrogant in the assessment of their moral capacity. As a gracious God, God effects with the law that which is alien to God (God's alien work) in order to arrive at what is proper to God (God's proper work).

The preaching of the law alone, however, does not lead us to true repentance or to belief in the gospel. God's Spirit must work together with the preached word so that we are able to experience the gospel. When the law convinces humans of their sin and they perceive the wrath of God, it drives them to despair. If people hear only the law, they remain in their despair and do not experience salvation. It is therefore important that the word of the gospel be added to the law, so that people realize that the law is not God's last word but rather points to God's forgiveness and salvation. The law precedes the gospel, so that humans find the gospel and, so to speak, flee to Christ. There

---

6 Martin Luther, *The Third Disputation against the Antinomians* (1538; *LW* 73:197), concerning thesis 67.

are not, however, two gods, as believed by Marcion in the second century: one God of the Old Testament, who is responsible for law, and the other God of the New Testament, who offers us the good news of the gospel. Both law and gospel are the work of the same God.

1. LAW AND GOSPEL AS TWO MODES
OF GOD'S ACTION

The law is not exclusively to be found in the Old Testament, nor the gospel in the New Testament. The law includes everything that reveals to us our sin, accuses our conscience, and terrifies us, regardless of whether we encounter it in Christ or in Moses. Luther not only by *law* understands the expressed imperatives, meaning the accusing and condemning word of God, but is also able to characterize the Lord's Prayer as "full of the teaching of the Law," since one who prays it earnestly confesses that one has sinned against the law and is in need of repentance.[7] When we pray, for example, "Hallowed be your name," we also admit that we have not yet fulfilled this challenge to revere God's name. In this way the Lord's Prayer exercises on us the work of the law. Even the Decalogue meets us either as law or as gospel. For example, the first commandment, that "I am the Lord your God," can be understood as a comforting assurance that we have a God in whom we can trust. But if the emphasis is on "I am the Lord," then the same word of God can be experienced as a threat.

The preaching of the gospel, too, has this character because it can be understood as law or as gospel. The preaching of Christ, who should be our example, can take on the character of the preaching of the law, since it manifests the will of God that we are to fulfill. The proclamation that Christ is our example can become the gospel when we look at the one who sacrificed himself for us. Even the proclamation of Christ as redeemer can become the preaching of the law,

---

7 Martin Luther, *[Theses for] The Third Disputation of Dr. Martin Luther [Against the Antinomians]* (*LW* 73:58), thesis 17.

since redemption presupposes sin. Yet the gospel also testifies to the goodness of God. Humans recognize their ingratitude and contempt for the goodness of God, for which they remain indebted to God.

The recognition of sin comes either from the law in the strict sense, that is, from the biblical admonitions and prescriptions, or from the gospel, insofar as it becomes law. Whatever points toward my obligation and shows me that I remain guilty, that is the law. The word of God, consequently, cannot be divided into the words containing law and the words containing gospel, for it is one and the same word that the sinner encounters as law and as gospel. For instance, the center of the gospel, being the word of the cross, exposes human sin and lostness more deeply and painfully than any law could do. Nevertheless, one can give no other advice to those who have recognized their sin in the face of God's love than to point them to the crucified Christ, who bears the sins of the world and brings good news to the poor. This same Christ, to whom we find ourselves ever again indebted, is then preached as Savior, as the mediator between God and humanity and the comforter of the distressed. The gospel leads to repentance as well as to faith; it leads to despair and to peace. It is true that law and gospel have two distinct and contrary functions, but both are functions of the same word of God and occur simultaneously.

Faith is a movement from law toward gospel, a movement that cannot be reversed. As gospel, however, it is a word of comfort, and therefore the movement comes here to rest. The law is set aside by the gospel, but never vice versa. God and the Lord, to whose mercy we are indebted, never ceases to be merciful. The opposition between law and gospel in the life of the sinner indicates a transitional stage on the way to the original unity of the two. It also points to the paradoxical situation that Christians, who have not fulfilled the law and thus stand accused, believe nevertheless in the gospel and fulfill the commandment of God, despite their sinfulness. Until now, we have spoken only of sinners. But since Christians are sinners and saints at the same time, the question arises whether the law has a continuing function for Christians.

2. CHRIST AS THE END OF THE LAW?

We have seen that Christ is the end of the law. Through him, the will of God, which we are unable to fulfill on our own, is fulfilled vicariously for us. Christ has liberated us from the power of the law so that we are no longer delivered over to the wrath of God and to death. The law as the demand of God, which requires eternal separation from God and thereby death because of our sins, is now fulfilled. The law no longer applies for those who are justified inasmuch as it accuses and condemns for past offenses. But God's holy will remains in force for them. Yet Christians do not experience this as a requirement of the law, for they freely do that which the law requires. Through God's Spirit, who abides in Christians, they willingly fulfill the law. They no longer stand under the demands of God's law but live their lives in accord with it through an act of love brought about by the Holy Spirit. The law has recovered its original function. It no longer condemns, yet it continues to express God's will. This is the one side, which considers us as justified people if and as long as we conduct our lives in agreement with God's will.

Although the law meets believers as neither demand nor accusation, and to a certain extent no longer applies to them, it nevertheless has significance for them. First, Christians continue to live their lives on this earth. At the same time, as both believers and sinners, they live sometimes according to the spirit and sometimes, as Paul says, according to the flesh. To the extent that Christians still belong to their former humanity according to the flesh, the law cannot be invalidated for them but rather reigns accusingly over them. Christians live without the law but also under it. For them the law is partly invalidated and partly still valid.

For Christians the decisive event has already taken place, for they have been justified. Yet to the extent that they remain or turn back to their former selves, the law continues to exercise its spiritual or theological function over them and convicts them of their sins. It summons them to overcome their former ways of life. Luther makes this clear in his explanation of baptism: "It signifies that the old creature in us with all sins and evil desires is to be drowned and die through daily contrition and repentance, and on the other hand that daily a new person is to come forth and rise up to live before God in righteousness and purity forever."[8] The law serves to overcome the entrenched state of humans and prods them to continually struggle against that which leads them astray from God. On earth the struggle for cleansing from sin is never completely successful. We are on the way to fulfilling the law, but this goal will never be accomplished completely. Only at the resurrection will the law have fulfilled its task and be completely abolished. Concerning the theological function of the law for Christians, however, one must remember that they are already moved by the Spirit of God, and repentance is no longer something hateful and difficult for them but rather, as Luther says, "delightful and easy."[9]

Yet how do we know what we should do? Do not we as Christians also need the information transmitted through the law so that we can know the will of God? To this Luther has two responses:

1. If the Holy Spirit moves Christians, they no longer depend on the law. By the power of the Holy Spirit, Christians can establish a new Decalogue, as did Jesus and the apostles.[10] They need no spelled-out precepts, since the Spirit teaches them what to do.

2. Yet Luther qualifies this assertion, admitting that not all Christians possess such a measure of the Spirit that they can be their own lawmakers. In such individuals the flesh continues to struggle against the spirit and impedes a clear judgment about the content of God's will. For this reason, it is good for Christians that they orient themselves to the apostolic imperatives of the New Testament. For

---

8 Martin Luther, *The Small Catechism*, in Kolb and Wengert, *Book of Concord*, 360, in explanation of baptism.

9 Luther, *First Disputation against the Antinomians* (*LW* 73:100).

10 See Martin Luther, *The Theses for the Doctoral Examination of Hieronymus Weller and Nikolaus Medler* (September 11, 1535; *LW* 34:112–13), theses 52–58.

Christians, however, these are no longer law but rather apostolic commandments or directives.[11]

There is, therefore, no theological aspect of the law for Christians. Those who have been justified fight no longer against sin but struggle rather to live positive, Christlike lives. For them the New Testament instructions are important, for they lead Christians to a proper knowledge of good works. To this end, the Decalogue is also useful for Christians, not in its word-by-word formulation but in the continuing relevance of its content.

As we see in his catechism, Luther expounded the Ten Commandments, freely supplementing and applying them in agreement with biblical admonitions. The commandments are hence not only a mirror in which we recognize sin, although they retain this function for the Christian; they are also a much-needed and wholesome instruction in what God expects from us by way of good works. In contrast to the opinion of later Lutheran orthodoxy and of the Reformed tradition, there is, according to Luther, no so-called third use of the law, applicable to the one who has been justified. The commandment of God, not the law, provides the Christian with guidance on the right way to live.

Luther's emphasis on the distinction between law and gospel means for us Christians that we cannot forfeit the law, God's holy will, as guidelines for shaping our lives. The law first of all shows us our alienation from God and then leads us to the gospel as the liberating word of God that God is a gracious God who has reconciled us to him through Christ. From God's reconciliation with us follows our reaction according to the guidelines of God as he has announced them in God's will. Since as human beings we are not perfect and always fall back into our earlier conduct, we need to be startled by the confrontation with God's law, which then urges us again toward the gospel. Luther advocates neither a legalistic piety nor a moralistic

---

11 See here the distinction made by Paul Althaus (in the vein of Luther) between law and commandment in Althaus, *The Theology of Martin Luther*, trans. R. Schultz (Philadelphia: Fortress, 1989), 271–73.

merging of law and gospel. Rather, he shows realistically that even with our best intentions, we always get entangled with this world and therefore continuously need the mercy and forgiveness of God for a new beginning.

QUESTIONS FOR DISCUSSION

How, for Luther, does human law relate to the divine law?
What does it mean to say that the law "accuses" us?
How does Christ end the law?

CHAPTER SIX

The Two Ways in Which God Rules

After World War II Luther's doctrine of the two realms or the two kingdoms was severely criticized, especially from the Reformed side under the leadership of Karl Barth. Allegedly political, economic, and social problems were excluded from the influence of the church, and a quietist attitude was promulgated. Some even wanted to detect a line of thought all the way from Augustine to Luther and then to Adolf Hitler. Indeed, the Lutheran doctrine of the two kingdoms stands within a long tradition that has nothing to do with Hitler. Instead it can be traced back to the Gospels.

According to the Gospel of John, Jesus speaks of the kingdom of God (John 3:3), and on the other side of the prince of this world (John 12:31) and his area of influence. One could think here of the kingdom of God and of the realm of darkness, which are in battle with each other. On the other hand, Jesus says, according to Mark 12:17, "Give to the emperor the things that are the emperor's, and to God the things that are God's." With this saying the worldly domain is distinguished from the spiritual. We are again in two totally differently arranged domains in this world. Luther seems to refer to this in his writing *On Temporal Authority: To What Extent It Should Be Obeyed* of 1523. He writes, "God has ordained two governments: the spiritual by which the Holy Spirit produces Christians and righteous people under Christ; and the temporal, which restrains the un-Christian and wicked so that—no thanks to them—they are obliged to keep still and to maintain an outward peace."[1]

1. THE HISTORICAL ROOTS OF LUTHER'S DOCTRINE OF THE TWO KINGDOMS

Luther was a biblical theologian and keenly aware of what was happening around him. Moreover, he was a preacher who sought to preach the gospel. His faithfulness to the Bible and his acute sense for relevant contemporary issues led him to the doctrine of the two kingdoms. Luther knew that according to the testimony of the New Testament the redemption of the world was accomplished through the advent of Christ. The path back to God for God's fallen creation was cleared, and its completion was made possible. Yet he knew that sin and death would rule over the world until the final consummation of salvation. What was revealed in the life and destiny of Jesus continued to await universal implementation. The tension between the "already" and the persisting "not yet," most clearly expressed by Paul, was the starting point for Luther's doctrine of the two kingdoms.

Luther stood in the tradition of the Middle Ages, in which a christocratic understanding of the state was prevalent. The dominion of Christ was to be realized through human dominion. During the Reformation many leading theologians, and not only those coming out of sectarian circles, held such views. Martin Bucer, for instance, in his book *De regno Christi* (*On the Reign of Christ*), attempts to lay the foundations for a Christian ordering of society in England under the leadership of King Edward VI (1537–1553; r. 1547–1553). Bucer's ideas, however, were quite utilitarian, for the proposed legislation that was supposed to be inaugurated by the king resembled

---

1 Martin Luther, *On Temporal Authority: To What Extent It Should Be Obeyed* (1523; *LW* 45:91).

very much the social and political conditions already existing in England at that time.

Luther, however, was suspicious of every christocratic approach, whether it was to be implemented by the church or by the state. Already in 1518 in his *Explanations of the Ninety-Five Theses* he questioned whether it was possible for the pope to hold both a spiritual and a secular sword. The Bible, according to Luther, spoke only of one sword, the "sword of the Spirit" (Eph 6:17).[2] Luther concludes from this that a doctrine that claims two swords should be thrown into hell. But he was not the first to reject the idea that the pope was invested with two swords or two kingdoms. This doctrine, which was popular in the Middle Ages, held that Christ had entrusted the pope as his successor with the worldly and spiritual realm and that the pope gives the worldly realm to the emperor as a fiefdom while he himself administers the spiritual realm. But already William of Ockham (ca. 1285–1347) and Marsilius of Padua (ca. 1290–1342/43) indicated that this teaching was based on a questionable allegorical interpretation of Luke 22:38. Even in Luther's time criticism against this doctrine had not been silenced.

In 1520, however, Luther went beyond the traditional polemic against the teaching of the pope's two swords. In his writing *On the Papacy in Rome*, he took up the question whether the authority of the pope was of divine or human character. He concluded that the pope's authority was, beyond doubt, of a worldly and not a divine nature. But Luther was also aware that the external order and structure of Christendom could not be abandoned, even though this structure could not be equated with true Christianity, which is spiritual. Both aspects of Christianity, external structure and inner substance, must be clearly distinguished, yet they cannot be separated from each other, or in one form or the other held to be absolute and definitive. They belong together just as the soul belongs to the human body.

---

2 Martin Luther, *Explanations of the Ninety-Five Theses* (1518; LW 31:244), thesis 80.

It becomes clear here why Luther moved ultimately toward a doctrine of two kingdoms with two entirely different structures. He was concerned about the inner spiritual life of Christianity and believed that, without a genuine distinction between the secular and spiritual realms, the latter would be overwhelmed in the long run by the worldliness of medieval christocracy. The distinction between the two kingdoms serves to make possible the proclamation of the gospel, unhindered by secular interests. On the other side, this distinction has thwarted the attempt of enthusiasts to spiritualize the world and to erect in the present world a "kingdom of God."

Since the historical situation had changed since the time of Augustine, Luther was unable to follow the two-kingdoms doctrine of Augustine in the development of his argument. For Augustine, Christians were still a small group of people who were under constant threat from the all-powerful pagan state.[3] Therefore Augustine equated the kingdom of the world with the realm that had fallen away from God. For him, this kingdom contained antigodly tendencies and could sometimes even be called the city of the devil. As we see in Luther's work *On Temporal Authority*, Luther initially largely accepted this view. Humanity must be divided into two groups. One group consists of the true believers in Christ, who realize the kingdom of God under the headship of Christ. The other group has no Christians in its midst and is the kingdom of the world and of the law. The world is essentially a sinful place in which Christians suffer as a small minority. It is the enemy of God and is ruled by secular princes. But Luther soon abandoned the Augustinian distinction, which had become outdated. In Luther's new version, the worldly kingdom included not only the state but everything that we view today as secular, such as marriage, property, vocation, and so forth. Since it contained everything we need for our livelihood, it

---

3 Even after Emperor Constantine (ca. 285–337, r. 306–337) had adopted the Christian faith and suspended the persecution of Christians, the majority of the influential families in Rome defended their traditional religion.

was now understood as something good and which also stood under God's rule.

2. THE UNITY OF THE TWO WAYS IN WHICH GOD RULES THE WORLD

It would be wrong to equate Luther's teaching of the two kingdoms with his doctrine of the kingdom of God and of the devil. Although he was absolutely convinced of the opposition that existed between God and the devil, as aforementioned, Luther did not think in dualistic categories as we find them sometimes in the Gospel of John. When Luther distinguishes between the kingdom of Christ and the kingdom of this world, the latter witnesses to the ordering and conserving will of God. This shows up, for instance, in the orders of nature and the political legal orders. Luther acknowledges the world as God's good creation but does not romanticize it as a perfect world. In contrast to the Gospel of John or to Augustine, Luther does not see the destructive work of the devil as being confined to the kingdom of the world or to the secular realm. The battle lines are now drawn through both kingdoms, and Satan seeks to transform them both into a God-opposing chaos. Luther confesses, "Against this rule of God, however, Satan rages; for his sole purpose is to crush and destroy everything that God creates and does through this rule."[4] It is God's will that both kingdoms or means of governing serve as bulwarks against the destructive attacks of the devil. This points also to the inner unity of the two kingdoms, as Luther writes:

> God has established two kinds of government among men. The one is spiritual; it has no sword, but it has the Word, by means of which men are to become good and righteous, so that with this righteousness they may attain eternal life. He administers this righteousness through the Word, which he has committed to the preachers. The other kind is worldly government, which works through the sword so that those who

---

4 Martin Luther, *Lectures on Zechariah* (1527; *LW* 20:173), on Zech 1:7.

do not want to be good and righteous to eternal life may be forced to become good and righteous in the eyes of the world. He administers this righteousness through the sword. And although God will not reward this kind of righteousness with eternal life, nonetheless, he still wishes peace to be maintained among men and rewards them with temporal blessings.[5]

This quotation from 1526 clearly shows that the same God stands behind both kingdoms and is active and present within both in different ways. Since God is active in both kingdoms according to his goodness and love, Luther concludes that God bestows a twofold blessing on humans: a material blessing for this life and a spiritual blessing for life eternal. We can see, therefore, an expression of God's love in the unity that exists between the two kingdoms.

This unity, however, is not only to be understood theocentrically. Luther also says that God has "three outward rules and in addition three outward ways or means for his own divine rule."[6] Elsewhere he writes, "God has therefore established three hierarchies against the devil: the family, the political order, and the Church."[7] Although God's lordship ultimately ties the two kingdoms together, the unity is also visible in human activities since humans live simultaneously in both kingdoms and in all three hierarchies. As responsible coworkers with God, humans encounter both forms of God's government, namely, God's *law*, as it comes to expression in the political realm, the family, and ecclesial structures, and God's *gospel*, as it is proclaimed to them in the preached word.

While both ways of ruling sometimes permeate the other, one should not simply merge them, as occurred more than once in the course of history.[8] A sad example is the struggle of investiture in

---

5 Martin Luther, *Whether Soldiers, Too, Can Be Saved* (1526; LW 46:99–100).

6 Luther, *Lectures on Zechariah* (LW 20:172), on Zech 1:7.

7 Martin Luther, *Die Zirkulardisputation über Matth. 19,21* (1539; WA 39/II:42.3–4), thesis 52.

8 Emperors had been heavily relying on bishops for their secular administration. On account of their official celibacy, they were not hereditary or quasi-hereditary nobility with family interests. Whatever they administered remained intact.

the eleventh and twelfth centuries, a political conflict between the nobility and the church over the ability to choose and install bishops (investiture), abbots of monasteries, and the pope himself. Through this struggle both powers were weakened in their own realm. The worldly authority lost political power and the spiritual authority gained worldly power but lost spiritual substance.

3. THE DISTINCTION AND MUTUAL PERMEATION OF THE TWO KINGDOMS

Although Luther was convinced of the fundamental unity of the two kingdoms, he never tired of emphasizing that we dare not merge them but must distinguish properly between them. The worldly and spiritual kingdoms must be distinguished as clearly as heaven and earth. The one is concerned with faith and eternal salvation, the other with external peace and the prevention of evil. The secular kingdom serves the earthly life and is finite, just as our life on earth, while the spiritual kingdom is related to life eternal, which is the ultimate goal of God's activity and is unlimited by time.

The worldly kingdom is ostensibly subordinated to the spiritual kingdom. God rules in the secular realm with the left hand, while God reigns over the spiritual kingdom with the right hand. This is God's actual work, and he cannot allow anyone else to reign over our souls. Christians are indeed aliens in the kingdom of the world, for they are guided by faith. Yet those who are not Christians cannot be guided by faith and love. They belong to the kingdom of the world and are instructed in proper conduct by earthly rules and by the sword. Because Christians are already leading their lives as the sword—that is, the worldly order—requires, the keeping of laws within the secular realm poses no difficulty for them.

Luther correctly observes that Christians cannot escape from the kingdom of the world; we "are all caught within it, indeed, born into it, before we become Christians. Therefore we must also remain within it so long as we live upon the earth, but according to the external bodily life and existence."[9] According to our worldly needs, we are citizens of the kingdom of the world, but according to our spiritual existence, we are citizens of the spiritual kingdom. This demonstrates that despite all their differences, an organic and mutual permeation of the two kingdoms exists.

Luther especially emphasizes one point at which our dependence on the kingdom of the world is manifest when he says that the spiritual kingdom requires peace and order in the world, which are results of the secular realm, in order that the word and the sacraments can be properly administered. Christians cannot lead a sheltered existence and escape from the world. This dependence is further made clear in the encompassing character of the worldly kingdom. As we have seen, the kingdom of the world encompasses not only human authority, government, and the orders of nature, but also the means that sustain our life on earth, such as marriage, family, property, business, and different vocations. These various human undertakings are carried out according to the law, or according to the sword, which are for Luther synonymous.

But how can one know the divine law if one is not even a Christian? Luther himself admits realistically that already "since the beginning of the world a wise prince is a mighty rare bird, and an upright prince even rarer."[10] Luther even writes that princes, for the most part, have been the greatest fools and the worst scoundrels. How, then, can they know the law of God to execute their function as rulers? Here we must once again recall the great trust Luther placed in natural reason, which God has given to all persons. The kingdom of the world is ruled through reason, and political and economic decisions are not made according to the Bible but according to reason. Luther observes that Christ never preached about economic issues but left this field to reason so that it could instruct us as to how goods should be divided and trade

---

9 Martin Luther, *Wochenpredigten über Matth. 5–7* (1530–1532; WA 32:390.15–18), in sermon on Matt 5:38–42.

10 Martin Luther, *Temporal Authority* (LW 45:113).

conducted.[11] Luther's understanding of reason, however, does not correspond to the Enlightenment conception, which understood reason as the autonomous possession of humans. For Luther, even natural reason is a gift of God, the proper use of which humans are ultimately accountable to God for.

The function of reason in Luther's doctrine of the two kingdoms is clarified when we turn to the distinction between general and special revelation. It is obvious for Luther that God has revealed certain things to all people through general revelation, while other things are only accessible through the special revelation in Jesus Christ. The regulations and laws of this world are not given through Christ but are already available through natural law, which is a source of general revelation. Luther is aware that in this world the knowledge of the will of God, which is made possible through general revelation, is often distorted and obscured as a result of human sinfulness. Yet he is convinced that it is not Christ but rather the law of each particular nation that answers the social and cultural questions concerning what a parent, teacher, politician, or judge should do in certain situations.[12] Of course, these laws are historically conditioned and have undergone many revisions. Luther challenges us, therefore, to use our reason to investigate whether these historically evolved laws still constitute an adequate expression of the natural law that they are supposed to represent.

Luther does not equate the natural law with the laws of a particular nation. The natural law, moreover, is the wellspring from which the other laws flow and on which basis they are to be criticized and interpreted. Yet we normally encounter the natural law in the form of a positive law, which we find in the laws and customs of a particular nation. Although Luther distinguishes between the positive law of a given nation and natural law, he sometimes identifies the

---

11 See the illustration given by Luther in *Wochenpredigten über Matth. 5–7* (*WA* 32:304.21–32), in sermon on Matt 5:1–3.

12 See Luther's distinction between the worldly and spiritual regiments, along with all the examples he provides, in *Lectures on Zechariah* (*LW* 20:172), explanation of Zech 1:7.

two—an identification that, in light of human sinfulness, is not without problems. Throughout history the legislation of a particular country often has not done justice to individuals or to the community in that country.

4. CHRISTIAN EXISTENCE IN THE SECULAR WORLD

Luther consistently maintains that Christians can and should be responsible citizens. Although Christians should not exercise any secular authority among themselves, they must make use of this authority in order to achieve and to preserve peace for others. For themselves, however, they should simply obey those who exercise worldly power, thus submitting themselves to secular laws. Luther also believed that Christians should not oppose evil if this opposition benefits only them. When Christians, however, occupy a secular office, for example as a parent, teacher, politician, judge, and so forth, they must oppose evil to the extent that this opposition is a function of their office. Otherwise, they would neglect their responsibilities and in the long run endanger others. We have the responsibility to enforce the rules connected with our positions with the necessary resolution, yet in love. For example, I must help the neighbor who is in difficulty, and when I am a judge and someone has injured another person, I must punish the culprit to the full extent of the law. But even as a lawbreaker, the person who injured my neighbor remains my brother or sister. Evildoers must indeed be punished and their crimes condemned, but the punishment must be executed with compassion. This means that I must distribute punishment only in my role as judge and not as a private individual. I enforce the law out of my responsibility toward God's own order, not because I hate the lawbreaker. Any feeling of vengeance or triumph has no place.

The validity of the law is not limited to the worldly realm but also has its appropriate place within the spiritual kingdom, yet only as a function of an office in which the law represents God and his order.

The law should never be degraded to a means for personal revenge, because it must ultimately be an act of love toward our neighbor. Luther can therefore encourage Christians to seek secular offices. If princes, masters, and judges are in need and one feels qualified to fill one of these positions, then one should strive to achieve this office; otherwise the necessary authority of the office would be held in contempt and weakened. Although Luther counsels against using force either too freely or too sparingly, he admits: "To err in this direction . . . and punish too little is more tolerable, for it is always better to let a scoundrel live than to put a godly man to death."[13] Just how far Luther distanced himself from the idea of a power-hungry secular order can be seen in his advice that Christians who hold secular office should imitate Christ. Just as Christ as supreme prince came and served us without seeking to increase his own power and honor, Christians in their offices should also not strive for their own advantage but serve those placed under their authority, protecting and defending them.

Luther's attitude toward property serves as a good example of his understanding of the service-oriented lifestyle of Christians. Luther maintains that all property, with the exception of that which is needed for personal use, is unjustly possessed and has actually been stolen from God, and therefore should be used to help others.[14] God demands of us to give generously to others. Maintaining possessions becomes theft when we do not use all the resources that go beyond our personal needs to alleviate the suffering of others. Luther, therefore, criticizes merchants who take interest from hardworking people.[15] Without the slightest investment of their own and without concern for others, they profit from diligent, hardworking men and women who are exposed to a variety of dangers in their work. To alleviate this injustice, Luther proposes that those who advance a

---

13 Luther, *Temporal Authority* (*LW* 45:104–5).

14 Martin Luther, *Predigten des Jahres 1522* (*WA* 10/III:275.7–10), in sermon on Luke 16:1–3 on August 17, 1522.

15 As we will see later, at Luther's time interest rates were exorbitantly high.

loan receive no set annual amount of interest but rather a percentage of the profits earned by the one who took out the loan. If the profits are high, then both will fare well. But when they are low, then both will suffer. In this way those who loan money can exhibit a genuine interest in the people to whom they have made a loan and in their work. Here again Luther's emphasis on the service-oriented nature of secular structures can be seen. These structures should serve people and not the free-reigning power of capital.

Luther emphasizes serving others with particular clarity when he describes the principles according to which (Christian) princes should exercise their office.[16] They must in the first place turn to God with good faith and deep prayer. Then they must treat those under their authority with love and an attitude of Christian service. Third, they must meet their counselors and officials with a spirit of openness and nonpartisan opinion. Finally, they should confront evildoers with responsible force and severity. These arguments show that although one cannot serve both God and mammon (or wealth), one can serve both God and emperor. It even appears that one can better serve the emperor in the secular realm if one also serves God in the spiritual realm. Yet one might rightly inquire to what extent Luther's position goes beyond a simple advocacy of the status quo and strives for a transformation toward a more just society. In other words, is the order of society advocated by the Reformer Luther not largely conservative, and does he not try to maintain the tradition in which he grew up?

Critique of the Two-Kingdoms Doctrine

As already mentioned, Lutherans have faced the accusation that the doctrine of the two kingdoms supports the status quo and hardly allows for any creative innovation. Of course, Luther's doctrine of two kingdoms should not be uncritically applied to our own day, just as Augustine's concept of a city of the world and a city of God

---

16 See. for the following Luther, *Temporal Authority* (LW 45:126).

could not be applied to the late medieval situation without decisive modifications. The modern form of societal structure in which the authority to govern comes from the people was unknown to Luther. His emphasis on the sword, that is, on force, and punishment through rulers must therefore be seen today as outdated. In the Western world, public order can be maintained only through a basic consent that must, however, be oriented toward specific values and objectives. In this regard Luther's insistence on order, justice, and mutual concern is certainly of continuing value.

It is precisely the ordering function of authorities, however, that has been met with much criticism in light of the rule of injustice in the Third Reich, as well as by the communist regime in East Germany, which existed in the heartland of the Reformation. Was not Luther's doctrine of two kingdoms partly responsible for the rise of the Third Reich? A clear answer to this question is not that simple. Hitler's movement started out in the predominantly Roman Catholic city of Munich, which was then called "the Capital of the Movement" (*Hauptstadt der Bewegung*), since there the National Socialist German Workers Party was founded in 1919, whose leader Hitler became two years later. Only much later did his movement engulf Protestant Prussia and in 1933 took over the government in Berlin, the capital of Germany. One should also consider that the Lutheran nations of Scandinavia offered resistance to the Nazi occupation, albeit with little success. Indeed, so many factors came into play with the rise of the Third Reich that one cannot simply lay the blame directly on the Lutherans. Additionally, one must also understand Luther's emphasis on order historically. Over against the medieval feudal system and its spread of terror, Luther stressed the king's peace and its preservation through every available means. One cannot speak either of a pure pacifism or of quietist inaction in regard to Luther. One should also not forget that, unconcerned about his own safety, Luther quite often appealed to the (Christian) conscience of rulers if they committed actions that Luther felt were inappropriate. A good example are Luther's publications during the Peasants' War.

With his writing of 1525 *Admonition to Peace on the Twelve Articles of the Peasants in Swabia*, Luther appealed to the conscience of the nobility to take seriously the social and ecclesial concerns of the peasants. But when the grievances coalesced into an insurrection of the peasants, Luther published in the same year his writing *Against the Murderous, Thieving Hordes of Peasants*, in which he demands that the worldly authority should take strict measures against the insurrectional peasants. Yet when this move of the nobility ensued in merciless slaughter of thousands of peasants, Luther wrote another pamphlet, *An Open Letter on the Harsh Book against the Peasants*. In this he justifies the hard measures against the peasants, but also writes that these measures should only serve to institute order and punish the evildoers, not be a means of vengeance. After this, "they were to show grace, not only to those whom they considered innocent, but to the guilty as well."[17] For their cruelty they will be held accountable by God on judgment day. Luther even calls such bloodthirsty knights "beasts." Luther did not pursue a party line but addressed the conscience of both those in authority and the peasants. Three points were important to him: (1) The subjects should not be exploited but treated with dignity. (2) Any insurrection should be punished with appropriate measures. (3) The worldly authority is not allowed to use vengeance against its subjects.

As a second point of criticism against Luther's two-kingdoms doctrine is the charge that this doctrine often contradicts the New Testament understanding of the kingdom of God. For this reason one is particularly inclined in Reformed circles to replace the two-kingdoms view with the reign of Christ in the one kingdom Jesus announced. Although such terminology can make very good sense inasmuch as it is oriented to the New Testament Gospels, it must not be forgotten that true believers, nominal believers, and unbelievers live with one another in the same world. Christians do not yet enjoy an eschatological community of believers, even if the New

---

17 Martin Luther, *Open Letter on the Harsh Book against the Peasants* (1525; *LW* 46:84).

Testament understanding of the kingdom of God presents this as having already been inaugurated. If one does not wish to make the church into a duplicate of the world, or vice versa, and place society christocratically under the explicit reign of Christ, then one must distinguish between that realm of society that allows itself expressly to be governed by God's word and all other areas, in which God is not mentioned or is even deliberately excluded and that must therefore be governed by God in an indirect manner.

Abiding Value of the Two-Kingdoms Doctrine

Despite all the criticisms, four aspects of Luther's doctrine remain especially important for us today and dare not be neglected:

1. The world is not only a place of sin and evil, but it stands also under the rule of God. To simply write off the world as bad not only goes against the prevailing sentiment of most people today but also contradicts the conviction of the Bible. The description of this earth as a valley of trouble, drudgery, and tears, and as the domain of the devil from which Christians will be delivered when they reach heaven, represents only one aspect of the biblical truth. If one sets up this partial truth as absolute, one gets the impression that the gospel cannot say anything positive about the world. Yet it is the understanding of the Old as well as the New Testament that God cares for this fallen world, protecting and preserving it.

Luther's emphasis on the reign of God within the secular realm reminds us that the world, even in its God-alienated state, is not without God. God's presence in the self-disclosure in Jesus Christ is merely the special way in which God is with his creation. If we reject the notion of a general revelation, which in hidden and faint ways always expresses itself in specific situations, we deny the divinity of God. The result would be an unbiblical, dualistic worldview in which the world, as it were, would exist without God. Humans, however, have always had an awareness of God and a concept of good and evil. Apart from some kind of a God-awareness or a general revelation, it would be difficult to explain the persistent religiosity of humans, through which religious themes continue to occupy our attention despite the secularization of our world.

2. *If we do not want to perish with the world, it must be a place of mutual concern and compromise.* Natural law, which Luther correctly saw expressed in the golden rule, is fundamental for the survival of a society. If the golden rule is denied as the fundamental principle of community life (for instance, in the family, in a nation, or in the whole of humanity), then human relationships will suffer in the long run. This can be recognized in the state capitalism of former socialist countries where now one often finds a small group of oligarchs, as well as in Western-style individualistic capitalism. Both forms of life together show too little mutual consideration and concern for fellow human beings who are destitute. In both cases society is not able to bear the long-term results.

The increasingly obvious north-south discrepancy on our globe functions in a similarly disturbing fashion. One can even demonstrate that humans ultimately destroy themselves if they do not exhibit sufficient care for creation as a gift of God but rather only selfishly exploit its resources. Present-day climate change points in this direction. Natural law functions as regulator in order that we might recognize our own exploitative tendencies toward other humans and toward nature and correspondingly correct them. Since humans are creatures blessed with reason, there is also cause for optimism that we will not mutually and permanently destroy our God-given environment in which we live but rather live peacefully with one another on the earth. Yet in our striving for mutual concern, we should realistically remember that the earth is only God's worldly realm, and that dreams of heaven on earth are utopian and unjustified even if pontificated by politicians and religious leaders.

3. *Power always brings with it a demonic temptation toward its misuse.* In contrast to many great religious figures both before and after him, Luther was very much aware of this temptation. When Luther chided evil princes and held their abuses before them, he knew that humans were by their sinful nature centered on themselves; they were

estranged from God. For this reason Luther turns often to Christian princes and encourages Christians in general to take up public office. Although Christians know the natural law and are willing to obey it, they are not guided by its precepts, which are often only hazy. If they truly follow Christ, they live according to the example of Christ and by his grace. Therefore they can establish signs and pointers to God's will in a demonic world. As the community of the body of Christ, their aim is to proleptically actualize the future provided by Christ. They need not despair because they are only a minority or because no one seems to take notice of their efforts. They can and must announce the future that Christ has provided, because they know the One who was the first to live as God intended humans to live. Therefore, both symbolically and literally, they should represent mutuality in their communal structures.

Christ has overcome the disunity and contradictory ways of humanity by dying the death of this world and inaugurating new life. Yet at present Christians can realize this new life only in a fragmentary fashion. They actively and anticipatorily await with the whole creation the universal coming of the new creation and the final redemptive act of God. At this future point the two kingdoms or forms of God's administration will be fused into God's one world, God's kingdom. In the contemporary world, however, we continue to live within two distinct kingdoms.

4. Luther always had a healthy mistrust of authority. In contrast to the Anabaptists, Luther did not close himself off from the world but called instead for Christian engagement within the world. Hence his criticisms of the sociopolitical relationships of his time were not destructive and did not reflect a mistrust of the ruling powers as such, but he was always conscious of his responsibility toward the entire community. He followed no particular party line. As mentioned earlier, during the Peasants' War he initially took up the complaints of the peasants who were being exploited by the nobility and upper classes and warned the ruling class, "For rulers are not appointed to exploit their subjects for their own profit and advantage, but to be concerned about the welfare of their subjects."[18] Yet he also warned the peasants, "The fact that the rulers are wicked and unjust does not excuse disorder and rebellion, for the punishing of wickedness is not the responsibility of everyone, but of the worldly rulers who bear the sword."[19] He warned both sides, "For God's sake, . . . take hold of these matters properly, with justice and not with force or violence and do not start endless bloodshed."[20] However, when the peasants took up arms, Luther reminded the princes of their duty: "For in this case a prince and lord must remember that according to Romans 13[:4] he is God's minister and the servant of his wrath and that the sword has been given to him against such people."[21] Christians, whether in a ruling position or as ordinary citizens, must therefore always look to what is right, take the side of what is right, and without resorting to violence seek to help that which is right to gain the victory, using all means at their disposal, so that the well-being of the entire community will be promoted.

In many of Luther's letters, he takes a stance regarding a political issue of his day. In so doing, he does not seek to become involved in political life by virtue of his reputation, as if he knows things better than others. Rather, he sees it as his Christian duty not to let the political events of the day pass by without comment. Luther almost always rejects advising anyone to resist the powers that be, although, as evidenced by his very clear criticisms, he does not seek to shelter them. Luther writes, if the governing authority minds the truth you offer, "well and good; if not you are excused, you suffer wrong for God's sake."[22] We owe the governing authorities the word of truth, whether that be criticism or affirmation, even though we should not count on its being accepted. Luther was convinced that

---

18 Martin Luther, *Admonition to Peace: A Reply to the Twelve Articles of the Peasants in Swabia* (1525; LW 46:22–23).

19 Luther, *Admonition to Peace* (LW 46:25).

20 Luther, *Admonition to Peace* (LW 46:40).

21 Martin Luther, *Against the Robbing and Murdering Hordes of Peasants* (1525; LW 46:52–53).

22 Luther, *Temporal Authority* (LW 45:124–25).

an irresponsible governing authority would not go unpunished, for God would bring down the powerful from their thrones and was able to "eradicate their roots along with their name and the memory of them."[23] God reigns and will in God's own good time abolish an insubordinate government.

Luther's fear that those faithful to the Roman church who rejected his reforms might brand him as a leader of rebellion also played a role in regard to his disapproving attitude toward opposing authority by force. He feared that under the pretext of putting down what they would label as "Luther's rebellion," they could roll back the reforms he had set in motion. In order not to give them any excuse to go on the offensive, Luther was very concerned to maintain order. This attitude had a lasting effect. For instance, it was very difficult for those influenced by Luther—such as lawyer Hans von Donanyi (1902–1945), lawyer and former Leipzig mayor Carl Friedrich von Goerdeler (1884–1945), and General Ludwig Beck (1880–1944)—to finally make the transition to active revolt in the July 20, 1944, attempt to overthrow Hitler. Following the thought of Luther, they understood Romans 13:2 ("Whoever resists authority resists what God has appointed, and those who resist will incur judgment") as a warning against every self-proclaimed uprising against authority. They asked themselves, therefore, whether Hitler could still be considered the legitimate authority. When they clearly saw that this was not the case and that their resistance would not result in chaos, they were ready to overthrow Hitler. Yet the coup was unsuccessful.

After the war, there appeared an important book on political ethics by Lutheran theologian Walter Künneth (1901–1997), *Politik zwischen Dämon und Gott* (Politics between the demonic and God).[24] Künneth portrays politics as existing in tension between Romans 13 (authority as the ordering power of God) and Revelation 13 (the demonic state), and concedes the right to rebellion against the state

---

23 Martin Luther, *Den 82. Psalm ausgelegt* (1530; WA 31/I:193.24–25).

24 Walter Künneth, *Politik zwischen Dämon und Gott* (Berlin: Lutherisches Verlagshaus, 1954).

under certain, carefully considered conditions. One should not, therefore, rise up against anything and everything in the opinion that, as a Christian, one knows better than others what is best for the common good. Luther himself had a healthy mistrust of attempts to Christianize the world:

> If anyone attempted to rule the world by the gospel and to abolish all temporal law and sword on the plea that all are baptized and Christian, and that, according to the gospel, there shall be among them no law or sword—or need or either—pray tell me, friend, what would he be doing? He would be loosing the ropes and chains of the savage wild beasts and letting them bite and mangle everyone, meanwhile insisting that they were harmless, tame, and gentile creatures; but I would have the proof in my wounds. Just so would the wicked under the name of Christian abuse evangelical freedom, carry on their rascality, and insist that they were Christians subject neither to law nor sword.[25]

Because there are sinful people in this world, even among Christians, one cannot dispense with a political authority that proceeds according to the principles of justice. But such a system needs the cooperation and engagement of Christians that these principles are maintained and no injustice can spread.

QUESTIONS FOR DISCUSSION

How does Luther's developed view of the two kingdoms differ from Augustine's?

What does it mean to say that God rules through both the law and the gospel?

How are our contemporary political situations (and our churches within them) similar and different from those of Luther's day?

---

25 Luther, *Temporal Authority* (LW 45:91).

CHAPTER SEVEN

Education Is for Everybody

Martin Luther was a multitalented person. He stood in the center of the Reformation, played the lute in his family circle, wrote hymns or set them to music, was skilled in carpentry, played chess, and loved Latin poets so much that he even took works of Plautus (ca. 245 BC–ca. 184 BC) and Virgil (70–19 BC) with him when he entered the monastery. For him "the languages are the sheath in which this sword of the Spirit [Eph 6:17] is contained."[1] With his translation of the Bible into German, he had an immense influence on the development of modern German, and many phrases in that language still date back to Luther. Nevertheless, for pastors knowing just German was not sufficient, in his estimate, and he cautions, "Who must preach and exegete Scripture and does not have the support of the Latin, Greek, and Hebrew language but will only do it with the mother tongue is prone to make quite some mistakes."[2] Therefore he emphasizes the necessity for pastors to have a good education, including a command of the ancient languages, something that today is still considered necessary for pastors in Germany. In order to educate pastors a

---

1 Martin Luther, *To the Councilmen of All Cities in Germany That They Establish and Maintain Christian Schools* (1524; LW 45:360).

2 Martin Luther, *Vom Anbeten des Sakraments des heiligen Leichnams Christi* (1523; WA 11:455.30–34).

reform of the universities was necessary, since many things were taught there that in his mind were not beneficial.

1. A GOSPEL-BASED EDUCATIONAL REFORM

In his 1520 writing *To the Christian Nobility*, Luther asserts that many writings of Aristotle, for instance on physics, metaphysics (i.e., theology), and ethics should not be taught at the university, since they are of little use and also do not help in understanding the gospel. But he says Aristotle's writings on logic, rhetoric, and poetry are useful to read, as well as Cicero's (106–43 BC) rhetoric, without the later commentaries. The main emphasis should rest on the classical languages, including Hebrew. Canon law, including the papal decrees, can be dispensed with. The sentences of Peter Lombard (ca. 1096–1164) and others, meaning collections of quotations by famous theologians on various theological topics, should not be taught at the beginning of theological studies but be reserved for the conclusion, and then only for future doctors of theology. Most important is the understanding of the Bible. To achieve this, education in schools was a must.[3] Luther writes, "The foremost reading for everybody, both in the universities and in the schools, should be Holy Scripture—and for the young boys, the Gospels. And would to God that every town had a girls' school as well, where the girls would be taught the gospel for an hour every day either in German or in Latin. Schools indeed!"[4] Luther's demand for Scripture alone and the priesthood of all believers presupposed sufficient education. But in medieval Europe illiteracy was still the norm. Just 5 to 10 percent of the population could read, and that usually only in the

---

3 One must remember that children were usually unpaid helpers at home or on the little farming plots people cultivated. Only boys from well-to-do families enjoyed some education, while girls usually had no education at all.

4 Martin Luther, *To the Christian Nobility of the German Nation Concerning the Reform of the Christian Estate* (1520; *LW* 44:205–6). For the reform of the universities, see 200–205.

cities. In the countryside the situation was even worse. The quest for education was therefore nonnegotiable if the Reformation should get a hold among the people.

In the face of the low educational standards, it was not surprising that both youth and laity had little knowledge of the gospel. Even most priests had little education. This became especially evident in the visitations of the congregations in Electoral Saxony during 1527–1528. As a remedy Luther composed in 1529 the *Wittenberg Hymnal* (*Wittenberger Gemeindegesangbuch*). In the same year his prayer book (*Gebetbüchlein*) was published, as well as *The Small Catechism* and *The Large Catechism*. The prayer book was not just a collection of prayers but was intended to introduce the Christian faith. The hymnal, too, was not merely a book in which one could learn the hymns needed for the liturgy but a comprehensive book for the songs of Christendom. The two catechisms were also not just intended to provide answers for catechetical instruction but introduced the praxis of Christian existence. The publications contained numerous pictures, like Luther's Bible translation. For Luther, word and picture belonged together, as well as music, because all three were instruments to instruct into the Christian faith, or more precisely into the faith of the Reformation.

Luther was an eminently practical person, and he knew that people could remember pictures much more easily than texts, and that a text sung could be more easily remembered than a plain text. Yet Luther was not just interested in reforming the church. Since the call for reforms of the church was issued largely from urban centers and from educated citizens, it was important for Luther that there existed a cooperation between church and school, not just for the educated but also for those with less schooling, so that they could understand and defend their faith. Luther accepted the traditionally stratified society. Important for him was always the idea of order, so that those standing in opposition to the Reformation could not accuse him of creating chaos by abolishing the notion of different classes in society. But when he insisted on education for everybody, he broke through the existing order into which one was born, such as nobility, citizens, or peasants. Ascending to a higher level in society was possible for everybody who had the necessary education. Therefore, Luther drove home to the territorial lords the significance of universities. Similarly, he admonished *The Councilmen of All Cities in Germany That They Establish and Maintain Schools*, as a 1524 publication is called. He demanded the possibility of education for everybody. Children of poor parents should be supported by scholarships given by cities or the church. Yet this support would lead to nothing if the parents did not allow their children in due time to acquire an education but kept them at home as unpaid servants. Parents also were to examine their children to see whether they were gifted and interested in attaining a higher education. Luther would not have approved of parents who sent children by all means to schools of higher education, as it is often the case today. This would overwhelm both children and teachers.

Once one has obtained a good education, one should not automatically demand a higher position than one had before. Luther interjects that it is of no disadvantage for a craftsperson to have learned Latin, since it is great if a person is learned, even though the office that could be associated with this education will never be available to this person.[5] Luther does not find that a different value adheres to different vocations, since fulfillment of life can be found in every vocation. If one does not succeed in climbing the social ladder, one is not disadvantaged. According to Luther, all human beings are children of God and should further the intellectual and physical gifts given to them by their Creator. These gifts should then be used to serve the others insofar as they need this service. Christians do not live and work for themselves but always for others.

In 1530, Luther confessed that *A Sermon on Keeping Children in School* "has grown to the point where it has almost become a book."[6] In the preface dedicated to the town clerk of Nuremberg, Lazarus Spengler (1479–1534), Luther emphasizes that even in a city such as Nuremberg there exists the danger that God's word and the schools

---

5 Martin Luther, *A Sermon on Keeping Children in School* (1530; LW 46:231).
6 Luther, *Sermon on Keeping Children in School* (LW 46:213).

will be neglected. It is often more important for parents that their children earn money than to attend school. They take their son from school and pretend that he can add and subtract and read books in German, and they think this is sufficient. But in a city such as Nuremberg there must be many kinds of people besides merchants.

It must have people who can do more than simply add, subtract, and read German. German books are made primarily for the common man to read at home. But for preaching, governing, and administering justice, in both spiritual and worldly estates, all the learning and languages in the world are too little, to say nothing of German alone. This is particularly true in our day, when we have to do with more than just the neighbor next door.[7]

For the different tasks in the state, the city, and the church, one needs well-educated people who, on account of the international exchange, know Latin, which was the common medium in which one conversed on the international level in the Middle Ages. Especially in Nuremberg, the city heavily invested in schools, and therefore the schools were not to be neglected.

2. EDUCATION FOR SPIRITUAL AND SECULAR MINISTRY

From the visitations in Electoral Saxony, Luther had learned that there were few pastors—usually former Roman Catholic priests— who were actually qualified for their office in both doctrine and general knowledge. For many former priests, their theological education consisted of having learned the sequence of the Mass from another priest, and they could only pray the Lord's Prayer in Latin. But there were also too few pastors altogether, since many had simply left their charge in the wake of the Reformation, and at times, especially during the Peasants' Wars, the whole educational system had nearly collapsed. In the Protestant territories

---

7 Luther, *Sermon on Keeping Children in School* (*LW* 46:215).

the monastery school had ceased to exist, and new educational institutions had to be established. Luther was afraid that in the near future three or four cities would just have one pastor, and ten villages only one chaplain, if the princes would not institute boys' schools and schools of higher education, and if parents would not send their children to these schools.[8] Moreover, many pastors were almost destitute, since the people no longer supported them, as they had done before with regard to monasteries in order to obtain merits before God. According to Luther, however, the real reason the pastoral office and preaching skills were in such disarray was that parents did not make their children learn. If children were gifted and loved to learn and their parents nevertheless did not allow them to attend school because they used the children at home as cheap servants, they were guilty of neglecting the pastoral office.

But pastors are also important for the worldly community. Luther explains, "For a preacher confirms, strengthens, and helps to sustain authority of every kind, and temporal peace generally. He checks the rebellious; teaches obedience, morals, discipline, and honor." For Luther, however, a preacher is not a replacement for the police, because "of all good things a pastor does these are, to be sure, the least." But Luther is mindful that preaching the law and reminding the people of the Decalogue are the tasks of a preacher. When a preacher neglects these, the moral order decays. Luther even reminds readers that worldly peace, "the greatest of earthly goods, . . . is actually a fruit of true preaching."[9] According to Luther, the pastoral office is an office to bring about peace. In this way a good pastor contributes to the well-being of people in body and soul. Even a king's son is not born too high to be trained for this office and work. One day God will demand an accounting from us what we have done with our children. Did we just educate them for temporal goods, or did we enable them to help those who need help?

---

8 See Luther, *Sermon on Keeping Children in School* (LW 46:234).
9 Luther, *Sermon on Keeping Children in School* (LW 46:226).

We should not surmise that for Luther schools serve only to educate pastors and teachers. He writes, "I do not mean that every man must train his child for this office, for it is not necessary that all boys become pastors, preachers, and schoolmasters." Luther is also not primarily concerned about children of townsfolk or of the nobility but about children of poor people. "Boys of such ability ought to be kept at their studies, especially sons of the poor. . . . Other boys as well ought to study, even those of lesser ability. They ought at least to read, write, and understand Latin, for we need not only highly learned doctors and masters of Holy Scripture."[10] According to Luther, education should be available to everybody, even if he primarily thought about possible education for the pastoral office. As aforementioned, one need not pursue this vocation. One can learn Latin and still become a craftsperson. According to Luther, higher education enlarges one's horizon, and one can always change to a different profession if one is needed and has the appropriate education.

Next to education for the pastoral office, Luther in this sermon focuses in a second and larger portion on education for the temporal authority, which maintains peace on earth as well as law and life. For Luther, "worldly government is a glorious ordinance and splendid gift of God," which God has instituted and established to maintain law and peaceful order for the people.[11] Princes and even the emperor usually do not have the ability to maintain law and order because they only use "fist and weapons," meaning force. But "heads and books must do it. Men must learn and know the law and wisdom of our worldly government," writes Luther.[12]

Those who maintain law in the temporal empire are jurists and scholars. Luther uses the term *jurists* comprehensively and includes chancellors, clerks, judges, lawyers, notaries, and all who have to do with the legal side of government. They maintain and help to further the whole worldly government if they exercise their office

---

10 Luther, *Sermon on Keeping Children in School* (LW 46:231).
11 Luther, *Sermon on Keeping Children in School* (LW 46:237).
12 Luther, *Sermon on Keeping Children in School* (LW 46:239).

properly, whether in towns, in the countryside, or at courts with the princes and with the emperor. If the parents seek their sons to be well-educated, then they also can "become such a useful person," and the money will be well invested.[13] This is not a purely private decision, because God has given certain people these children and goods so that they can serve God with them and therefore keep their children to service for God. Maintaining God's order and temporal authority is a divine service. For Luther, a temporal or secular task has become a divine calling in the same way as the exercise of the pastoral office.

Luther often complains about the decay of education. Educated people are needed in the cities as well as at court, and if they are not available as necessary, then "kings will have to become jurists, princes chancellors, counts and lords clerks, mayors sextons."[14] Since education to these good and useful works pleases God, and the service in these works is for God's sake, they are much more valuable than if one thinks just of one's own benefit and the money that children could earn without this education. Therefore preachers and teachers need to imprint this on the minds of the boys and the parents of these children from early on, that these stations and offices are instituted by God and are not to be treated with disrespect but kept in high honor. Ultimately they serve the peace and unity of humans. Many people, however, do not recognize how necessary and useful these offices are in the world. One should also not forget, writes Luther, that it is much easier to learn how to use armor than how to execute properly a learned office. In conclusion, Luther admits, referring to Aristotle:

A diligent and upright schoolmaster or teacher, or anyone who faithfully trains and teaches boys, can never be adequately rewarded or repaid with any amount of money. . . . If I could leave the preaching office and my other duties, or had to do so, there is no other office I would rather have than that of schoolmaster or teacher of boys; for I know that next to that of preaching, this is the best, greatest, and

13 Luther, *Sermon on Keeping Children in School* (*LW* 46:241).
14 Luther, *Sermon on Keeping Children in School* (*LW* 46:244).

most useful office there is. Indeed, I scarcely know which of the two is the better.[15]

Education in schools was extremely important for Luther. But he also remembered that before the Reformation set in, people liberally supported churches and schools so that one could send children to schools run by monasteries and to other schools. But since the Reformation, the willingness to donate money and interest in these schools had completely vanished. On account of this new situation Luther argued that temporal authorities must establish schools and urge people to send their children to school so that temporal offices could be staffed with well-educated persons. If a father was too poor to afford schooling for his son, then he must be supported with subsidies by ecclesial or worldly authorities.

Already in 1524 Luther wrote *To the Councilmen of All Cities in Germany That They Establish and Maintain Christian Schools*. Luther recalled that prior to the Reformation, many parents sent their sons and daughters into monasteries and cathedral chapters so that they no longer needed to take care of them.[16] They learned all kinds of arts in these institutions. But with the Reformation this custom broke off, and most young people no longer had a chance to learn intellectual or menial trades. This means the decay of the monasteries and ecclesial institutions was accompanied by a similar breakdown of education. This was not what Luther had intended, since he valued a good education. Therefore Luther told the cities that they should become the supporters of educational institutions. He showed them that annually they spent much money on maintaining the infrastructure by repairing roads, dams, bridges, and so on, necessary for urban living. Then he asked whether they should not spend as much money on poor, neglected youth. As a result of the Reformation they had saved a lot of money, since they no longer wasted "money and property on indulgences, masses, vigils, endowments,

---

15 Luther, *Sermon on Keeping Children in School* (LW 46:253).

16 This had been true for Luther's own wife, who even learned some Latin in the nunnery.

bequests, anniversaries, mendicant friars, brotherhoods, pilgrimages, and similar nonsense." Should they then not, asked Luther, "out of gratitude to God and for his glory, contribute a part of that amount toward schools for the training of the poor children?"[17] According to Luther, this would be an excellent investment and would express their thanks toward God that they had been liberated from all this superstition. Therefore Luther insistently pleaded with the council-men, for God's sake, to take care of the youth. Parents, too, were reminded of their responsibility.

3. THE DUTIES OF PARENTS

With reference to Psalm 78:5 (God "commanded our ancestors to teach to their children" [the glorious deeds of our Lord]), Luther asserted that it was the obligation of the parents to teach their children.[18] If the parents failed to do their duty, then it was the responsibility of the authorities and the city council to keep children in school. Languages and the arts helped people to understand Holy Scripture and to conduct temporal government. "If through our neglect we let the languages go (which God forbid!), we shall not only lose the gospel, but the time will come when we shall be unable to speak or to write a correct Latin or German."[19] The Reformation was largely propagated by pictures and writing. Therefore education in reading and writing was essential for the persistence of the Reformation. Because of the priesthood of all believers, it was also necessary that every Christian could read and understand the Bible.

For Luther, education was indispensable for the spiritual estate, but also for the temporal. Since "the temporal government is a divinely ordained estate," we must "get good and capable men into it." Though the Romans and the Greeks "had no idea of whether

---

17 Luther, *To the Councilmen of All Cities* (*LW* 45:350–51).

18 Luther, *To the Councilmen of All Cities* (*LW* 45:353).

19 Luther, *To the Councilmen of All Cities* (*LW* 45:360).

this estate were pleasing to God or not, they were so earnest and diligent in educating and training their young boys and girls to fit them for the task."[20] Luther even concedes that if we did not need schools for the spiritual estate, it would alone be reason enough to establish everywhere

> the very best schools for both boys and girls, namely, that in order to maintain its temporal estate outwardly the world must have good and capable men and women, men able to rule well over land and people, women able to manage the household and train children and servants aright. Now such men must come from our boys, and such women from our girls. Therefore, it is a matter of properly educating and training our boys and girls to that end.[21]

Since common people are incapable, unwilling, or ignorant of this task, and since princes and lords prefer to fool around and "are burdened with high and important functions in cellar, kitchen, and bedroom," this task of providing for the education the young rests with the councilmen alone. If these young people were instructed and trained in schools or other institutions, where learned and well-trained schoolmasters and schoolmistresses were available to teach the languages, "the other arts, and history," then they would receive a comprehensive education and could "take their own place in the stream of human events."[22]

If people were afraid that children therefore would no longer be available to help at home, Luther dispersed such worries, saying,

> My idea is to have the boys attend such a school for one or two hours during the day, and spend the remainder of the time working at home, learning a trade, or doing whatever is expected of them. In this way, study and work will go hand-in-hand while the boys are young and able to do both. . . . In like manner, a girl can surely find time enough to attend school for an hour a day, and still take care of her duties at home. . . . Only one thing is lacking, the earnest desire to train the young and to benefit and serve the world with able men and women. . . .

---

20 Luther, *To the Councilmen of All Cities* (*LW* 45:367).
21 Luther, *To the Councilmen of All Cities* (*LW* 45:367–68).
22 Luther, *To the Councilmen of All Cities* (*LW* 45:368–69).

> The exceptional pupils, who give promise of becoming skilled teachers, preachers, or holders of other ecclesiastical positions, should be allowed to continue in school longer, or even be dedicated for a life of study.[23]

Luther suggests here a dual track of education for the lowest level that provides skills in crafts as well as in the intellectual faculties. For higher education, he suggests either a more intensive intellectual education or one that is exclusively devoted to scholarship. While this dual-track education was new, even more revolutionary was Luther's insistence on education for both boys and girls. Moreover, in order to advance the students in education, Luther suggests that "no effort or expense should be spared to provide good libraries or book depositories, especially in the larger cities which can well afford it." Luther refers here to the libraries in monasteries and foundations. As time went on, there were few good books left among them. The arts and languages declined, and "there were no books available than the stupid books of the monks and the sophists."[24] Yet one should make judicious selections. First of all, the Bible should be available in different languages, then the best commentaries of the Bible in the classical languages, including those of the church fathers, then books that are helpful in learning the languages, then Christian and pagan poets so that people can learn the grammar. Also books in the liberal arts and all other arts should be available. Finally, books of law and medicine and especially chronicles and histories in different languages should be acquired. For Luther, libraries should be of help for all ways of life.

Philipp Melanchthon, Luther's collaborator in Wittenberg, was called the *Praeceptor Germaniae*, the "teacher of Germany," on account of his numerous and widely circulating textbooks, editions of ancient texts, translations, and commentaries, which were used even in Roman Catholic schools, yet without mentioning his authorship. For example, his Greek grammar of 1518 was so successful that it enjoyed more than forty editions. Luther had no time for or

---

23 Luther, *To the Councilmen of All Cities* (*LW* 45:370–71).
24 Luther, *To the Councilmen of All Cities* (*LW* 45:373, 375).

interest in writing textbooks for students as did Melanchthon. But he provided the theological foundation for the education of a Christian. Christians must be accountable for their faith before God and other people. This presupposes a solid education. Since they should lead responsible lives in the worldly realm, they need an education that develops intellectual as well as manual skills. For this the knowledge of God's will in regard to ethical conduct is indispensable.

Education in spiritual, intellectual, and manual matters pertains to both boys and girls. For a more challenging positions, a more intensive education is needed than for a less demanding one. Education depends on the gifts of the individual, and the exercise of a calling depends on the needs of society. Therefore a certain education does not always guarantee that one can work in a corresponding profession. For Luther this does not cause problems, since each calling, profession, or job is of equal value and is fulfilled in service for God and therewith in thanking God for his prevenient grace. Luther's emphasis is here on the service function of a profession and not on the remuneration one may obtain.

The education demanded and inaugurated by Martin Luther had unforeseen consequences for Lutheranism. Sociologist and economist Max Weber (1864–1920) noted a gap in prosperity between Roman Catholics and Protestants. Economists Sascha Becker (University of Warwick, Great Britain) and Ludger Woessmann (University of Munich) showed in a 2008 study that this gap did indeed exist in nineteenth-century Prussia.[25] It was not the work ethic that made Protestants more prosperous, as Weber thought, but greater proficiency in reading and writing. This is exactly the point Luther stressed. According to Luther, everybody should be able to read the Bible. But not only was the income of Protestants higher; on account of their better education, they also generally had a higher level of education than Roman Catholics. The reason for this was that for

---

25 Sascha O. Becker and Ludger Woessmann, "Luther and the Girls: Religious Denomination and the Female Education Gap in 19th Century Prussia," in *IZA Discussion Papers 3837* (Institute for the Study of Labor, 2008), 1.

a long time the idea prevailed in Roman Catholicism that higher education was primarily needed if one wanted to become a priest. For this purpose good schools were established in dioceses and in monasteries. But for intellectually gifted children of Protestants, a higher education was natural regardless of what kind of profession they wanted to pursue. This discrepancy in education was also noticeable for a long time at my home university of Regensburg, which is located in a predominantly Roman Catholic area. The majority of the professors were Protestant and predominantly hailed from northern Germany, where most people adhere to the Lutheran faith.

Luther's emphasis on education included both boys and girls, whereas with Roman Catholics it was usually only boys, even if they did not want to enter the priesthood later on. In the second half of the nineteenth century already in the first grades there were as many Protestant girls as there were boys. Studying the data from the first census in Prussia in 1816 and then again in 1871, Becker and Woessmann investigated the educational level of adults and found that Protestant women could read and write better than Roman Catholic men at that time.[26] This fact considerably improved the advancement of Protestant women. For instance, in 1908, the year in which women were for the first time allowed to study in German universities, there were eight times more Protestant female students than Roman Catholic female students in German universities.[27] Even in the 1970s, the gender gap in regard to education was considerably smaller in Protestant states in Germany than in predominantly Roman Catholic states.

Luther's emphasis on education for both boys and girls contributed to the equalization of education between Protestant men and women. Since then, however, Roman Catholics have largely closed this gap. But this does not diminish the significant influence the Lutheran Reformation had on education in Protestant areas.

---

26 Becker and Woessmann, "Luther and the Girls," 15.
27 Becker and Woessmann, "Luther and the Girls," 18.

QUESTIONS FOR DISCUSSION

How did Luther's call to universal education clash with established social norms?

Why did Luther stress the importance of education for poor children?

What is the value and role of education in today's culture and society?

CHAPTER EIGHT

A Calling Is Not Just for Priests

Similar to Luther's emphasis on education, his teaching concerning vocation has had an incredibly broad impact, extending well beyond the ecclesiastical and religious spheres. The term *vocation* as it is used in "vocational school" or in "my vocation as a teacher" is derived from the Latin *vocatio*, which means "calling." In the late Middle Ages in which Luther lived, *calling* was a strictly religious, ecclesial, and theological term that was applied to ecclesial offices and especially to being a monk. A monk was called and therefore had a vocation or a calling. Today the Roman Catholic canon law stipulates that through baptism all Christians, not just priests and monks, "are called to exercise the mission which God has entrusted to the Church to fulfill in the world" (204). While all Christians now have a calling through baptism, this is still restricted to activities within the mission of the church. In the New Testament Paul also talks about a divine calling that pertains to all Christians (Rom 11:29: "For the gifts and the calling of God are irrevocable"; 1 Cor 1:26: "Consider your own call, brothers and sisters"). Already in the first centuries this calling was narrowed down to pertain to priests and monks only. Luther then extended the concept of calling again by including secular activities, which are part of everybody's duties. He did not regard the so-called spiritual or ecclesial activities higher than the secular ones and rejected the prevailing notion that a monk was in some ways privileged.

For Luther there was no difference between a religious calling and a nonreligious activity, since all human activities are immediately related to God. Everybody has a calling or a vocation, which one fulfills in direct service to God. The combined influence of the Protestant church and the middle-class world of seventeenth- and eighteenth-century Germany produced an understanding of carrying out one's vocation as a direct service to God. Vocation became the focal point of the responsible activity of creative human beings. Vocational loyalty was understood not just as loyalty to one's employer but primarily as loyalty to God.

In the periods of the Enlightenment and German idealism in the late eighteenth and early nineteenth centuries, vocation ultimately became a fundamental concept in the ethical teaching about duty. Thus, according to philosopher Immanuel Kant, the universal moral law is fulfilled in one's vocation. For this reason Frederick the Great (1712–1786), who ruled Prussia as king from 1740 to 1786, proclaimed, "The prince is the first servant of his state." Following Kant, Protestant theologian Albrecht Ritschl (1822–1889) emphasized the significance of the term *calling* in talking about the vocation of a Christian. For him the term *calling* also showed that Christians who meet their calling in a loyal manner also help to realize the kingdom of God. This description of vocation as duty rubbed off on the Prussian officials and government workers, who were known for their conscientious fulfillment of duty. Prussia's supremacy in Germany led to the development of an efficient and incorruptible administration that, in the community of nations, is still to this day exemplary in many ways.

1. EVERY PROFESSION IS OF EQUAL VALUE

For Luther, of course, such far-reaching ramifications were unintended. In his teaching about vocation, he was primarily concerned to dispel the view common in his time that priests and monks, through their vocation within a spiritual order, possessed a higher level of sanctification than laypersons, who pursued a secular vocation. "Hence when a maid milks the cows, or a hired hand hoes the field—provided that they are believers, namely, that they conclude that this kind of life is pleasing to God and was instituted by God—they serve God more than all the monks and nuns, who cannot be sure about their kind of life."[1]

In his 1521 writing *On Monastic Vows*, Luther rejects the vocational privilege of monasticism, which held that monastics and priests had a vocational status superior to that of all others. From 1 Corinthians 7:20, "Let each of you remain in the condition in which you were called," Luther concludes that even an ordinary working person, without having to belong to a monastic order, can carry out here on earth an occupation that is good and commanded by God. If one is not sure about one's calling, Luther has a very simple answer:

> Then you may reply: "But if I am not called, what shall I do then?" Answer: How is it possible that you are not called? You will always be in some estate; you are a husband or a wife, or a son or a daughter, or a servant or a maid. Take the lowest estate for yourself. If you are a husband, and you think you have not enough to do in that estate with governing your wife, children, domestics, and property so that all may be obedient to God and that you do no one any wrong? Even if you had four heads and ten hands, you would still be too little to make a pilgrimage or to take some saint's work as your own.[2]

For Luther, vocation no longer means to be called out of the world to a better and higher vocational status, but is seen rather as a calling to and within that place where one does one's work. If one does one's work carefully, then one has no longer time for pilgrimages and other so-called holy activities.

Luther's rejection of the idea of a religious vocation being more worthy also follows from his conviction that all persons are justified,

---

1 Luther, *Lectures on Genesis* (*LW* 3:321), on Gen 20.
2 Luther, *Christmas Postil 1522* (*LW* 75:353–54), in sermon on John 21:19–24.

that is to say accepted, through trust in God, not by being able to demonstrate certain good works before God. Because we have already received everything from God our Creator, it would be a contradiction to want to be rewarded by God for one good work or another. Good works therefore have nothing to do with our justification. "The things we do for God are not called good works, but rather the things that we should do for our neighbor—those are good works."[3] That we perform works here on earth is first motivated by the fact that our fellow human beings need our help, that is, our works. Then those who perform some worldly task do it to thank God for what he has done for us, that he has accepted us by grace alone. Persons who do secular work do it to the glory of God and as a service to their neighbor. One should view even the pastoral office from this perspective, because here, too, service to one's neighbor and the glorification of God are expressed. There is no direct service to God, because there is only an indirect one through the neighbor to God. We must remember here the word of Jesus: "Just as you did it to one of the last of these who are members of my family, you did it to me" (Matt 25:30).

In our industrialized, urbanized, and largely anonymous society, however, this conception of vocation has largely disappeared. The modern understanding of one's job is characterized by maximizing investment and profit and by the ability to exercise control. But employers and employees today increasingly notice that without personal engagement, what is simply a job eventually amplifies the meaninglessness of life over the long run. Health problems, lack of motivation, and a decreasing quality of work are only some of the results. For more and more people, the level of remuneration and the shortness of the working week are no longer decisive, but what matters is that the work is interesting, challenging, and personally engaging. Therefore Luther's emphasis on vocation as service of one's neighbor takes on renewed significance today.

---

3 Martin Luther, "Sermon for the First Sunday after Easter," April 27, 1522 (*LW* 69:332), on John 20:21–23.

As we turn now to the task of briefly outlining Luther's understanding of vocation, we must first view it in light of his understanding of one's status or station within society, which to some extent parallels his understanding of vocation. Luther understands by vocation much more than work for which we get paid. It includes many stations in life, in family, at the workplace, in private or in public.

2. A STATION IS THE PLACE WHERE I PRESENTLY STAND

One cannot equate Luther's concept of station with the concept of class in the modern sense of the word. Rather, it encompasses "my present state." For Luther, one's station is first of all a general concept of order that makes it possible to group together all those persons who in one way or another share something in common that distinguishes them from all others. In 1630 German hymn writer Johann Heermann (1585-1647) penned words that reflect the thought of Luther: "Give me the strength to do with ready heart and willing whatever you command, my calling here fulfilling."[4] Such a calling or station could define a group (such as youngsters), a social class (such as peasants), or a churchly estate (such as monks). Luther sees the various stations (in German, *Stand*) as starting points for our actions. They are beyond our own arbitrary decisions, for the Creator has established them and placed us within a particular station. These stations are places to which God calls us so that we can carry out a specific and unique vocation as a teacher, a mother, or a child. Stations have a stabilizing function, but they cannot be compared to castes, which are closed in on themselves and do not allow any mobility from one station to another.

According to Luther stations are not static, but there is a certain mobility from one station to another. Medieval tradition generally recognized three stations: the teaching station, the economic station,

---

4 See *Evangelical Lutheran Worship*, hymn 806, stanza 2.

and the political station. For Luther one did not belong exclusively to one of these three stations. He explains in his lectures on Genesis: "This life is profitably divided into three orders: (1) life in the home; (2) life in the state; (3) life in the church. To whatever order you belong—whether you are a husband, an officer of the state, or a teacher of the church—look about you, and see whether you have done full justice to your calling."[5] These stations or orders to which we belong simultaneously describe the multidimensionality of life and the various interhuman relations that make up the structure of our existence. For Luther these are no worldly relationships but have deep religious significance, since we pursue our divine calling in the way in which we interact with other people and how we master the tasks of our daily life.

The economic station was for Luther first of all marriage, then the family in the narrower sense, that is, the community of parents and children, and also the family in the broader sense, including domestic servants as well. Finally, Luther was able to classify the socioeconomic and civic-societal relations of human beings under the category of the economic station. Of importance for Luther in regard to this station are the economic relationships of people who all belong to the same social structure with one another. For example, the union of husband and wife for the purpose of rearing children is as much a biological necessity as the procurement of food and clothing. It is important in regard to activities within this station that the laws of life are not disregarded and that the life of one's neighbor is improved.

The political station, too, is established by God, for God desires order in society. Service of the state includes not only governing but also obeying, which includes everybody who lives in a certain territory, both the governing authorities and the common people. While the laws of biology (in the station of the family) are unchangeable, the laws that lie at the foundation of the political station are changeable. Here one finds an order appropriate to each era that joins people together.

---

5 Luther, *Lectures on Genesis* (LW 3:217), on Gen 18:15.

In the case of the teaching station or the ecclesial station, neither the laws of biology nor the laws of the state are applicable. Instead, we encounter here specific functions, so that the teaching station has its own specific laws. To the teaching station do not only belong those who preach and administer the sacraments, but also the custodians who supervise the finances of a congregation, those who assist the full-time staff, and even common Christians. This means that for Luther all Christians belong to the teaching station, be it at home or in the church. We notice here quite different structures and relationships depending on which aspect of our lives and our activities we examine.

Luther writes, "God has instituted many estates in life in which men are to learn to exercise themselves and to suffer. To some he has commanded the estate of matrimony, to others the estate of the clergy, to others the estate of temporal rule."[6] Yet none of these estates or stations is higher than the others, and all have as their goal that they serve others. To be sure, each person is placed within a specific station, but one can also switch from one station over to another, for instance from the spiritual station to the political or the economic. Yet every station has its own difficulties, so none is better or easier than the other. There is also no station that is not contaminated by sin, for there is no station in which the command of God is fully carried out.

Why did God create and establish these stations in the first place? According to Luther, the stations embody the will of God so that God might provide for order and serve the needs of human beings through these external forms: "Without these masks [that is, stations] peace and discipline could not be preserved."[7] It is particularly important, to stress this point once more, that none of these stations is placed above or below the others. Luther strictly rejects a higher status for the spiritual station, for there must not exist any hierarchy of stations.

---

6 Martin Luther, *The Holy and Blessed Sacrament of Baptism* (1519; *LW* 35:39).

7 Luther, *Lectures on Genesis* (*LW* 7:184), on Gen 41:40.

Each of the stations is equally necessary for human life. A station, then, is the objective range of duties connected to a particular position within society. The term *station*, however, is no way a synonym for *vocation*. It denotes the situation or the location where I fulfill my calling or vocation.

3. EVERYBODY IS CALLED BY GOD

The word *vocation*, as I have indicated, is not another way of saying *station*. Vocation, to be sure, speaks of the same reality, but from a different perspective. The stations are universally objective structures, while vocations are objective structures only when the individual is permanently connected with a particular vocation and is personally obligated to it. For instance, every Christian belongs to the spiritual or ecclesial station, whether as a father who instructs his children in the Christian faith or as pastor who preaches the word of God and administers the sacraments. One is called to the pastoral office through human beings, who represent God by exercising the church's right to call an individual. People are called to marriage because we are created as male or female, to rear children and establish a household. The biological perspective of the station of the family and the individual's personal decision become intertwined. Likewise, the station of a prince or that of a subject becomes a vocation inasmuch as a specific directive is given to a person to take up the tasks bound to this calling. A certain calling comes from God, who selects a person for a certain task and thereby calls that person.

Vocation as Divine Service

Belonging to a particular station does not automatically guarantee that carrying out the functions of that station will be divine service, that is, that it will correspond to the divine will. Luther never gets tired reminding us that every calling has a service character. For instance, a government is instituted for those who are governed and not for those who govern (to enrich themselves). A pastor works for a congregation, for the faithful. This means we do not choose a vocation or calling to see how much we get and how little we need to invest for this calling. We do not carry out our calling for ourselves but for other people. If humans properly fulfill their calling, they are coworkers with God regardless of whether they are Christians. We are coworkers in the continuous creative activity of God through which God sustains the world and everything within it, including we who live in this world.

A station becomes a calling if it is appropriately executed and serves other people. One can simultaneously have different callings, not just the one that today is usually understood as one's vocation or work, since one gets remunerated for doing this, but also the calling within the biological order as father, mother, son, or daughter. For Luther one cannot distinguish between a calling or a work that is performed according to certain rules, and the more intimate sphere of interhuman relationship where we conduct ourselves in Christian love. Wherever we encounter persons and tasks, God summons us to exercise our calling appropriately in Christian love and according to the best of our abilities. Luther explains this in his lectures on Genesis:

> Thus every person surely has a calling. While attending to it he serves God. A king serves God when he is at pains to look after and governs his people. So does the mother of a household when she tends to her baby, the father of household when he gains a livelihood by working, and a pupil when he applies himself to his studies, who steeps himself in his work, a student who diligently studies. . . . Therefore it is great wisdom when a human being does what God commands and earnestly devotes himself to his vocation without taking in consideration what others are doing. But surely there are few who do this.[8]

Luther is not naive. He knows that people are inclined to compare themselves with others. Therefore, he admits: "There are very few who live satisfied with their lot. The layman longs for the life of a cleric,

---

8 Luther, *Lectures on Genesis* (*LW* 3:128), on Gen 17:9.

the pupil wishes to be a teacher, the citizen wants to be a councilor, each one of us loathes his own calling, although there is no other way of serving God than to walk in simple faith and then to stick diligently to one's calling and to keep a good conscience."[9] He warns that God "does not want people to change or abandon their vocations, as under the papacy it was considered piety to have given up one's customary way of life and to have withdrawn into a monastery."[10]

Since God rarely interferes directly in this world, he wants to prepare his gifts through our work, and we become "the masks of God, behind which He wants to remain concealed and do all thing."[11] This means that all useful occupations are certified by God, without which a city or a state cannot exist. If we were to neglect them we would actually neglect God's calling and avoid that to which we have been called. For Luther a calling is therefore God's call to us to discern in a given situation what God expects from us. A calling or vocation, whether we get paid for it or not, is more than a means to earn money. It is a way in which God maintains and furthers other people through us, and beyond that the common well-being. Regardless how the different callings or vocations may look to the outside, in themselves they are all the same, since they are instituted by God to maintain and further God's creation.

Helping our neighbor, being a parent, and rearing children demonstrate a commonality in our calling whereby the differences between rich and poor and between those in authority and those under authority disappear. "Everybody should lead a life of which he knows that it is pleasing to God even if it be despised and lowly. A servant, a maid, a father, a mother, these are the forms of life which have been instituted and sanctified through the divine Word and are well-pleasing to God."[12] It is an important element of Luther's concept of vocation that every genuine vocation, being derived from a

---

9 Luther, *Lectures on Genesis* (*LW* 3:128), on Gen 17:9.

10 Luther, *Lectures on Genesis* (*LW* 3:63), on Gen 16:7–9.

11 Martin Luther, *Selected Psalms* (1532; *LW* 14:114), on Ps 147:3.

12 Martin Luther, *Lectures on Isaiah* (*LW* 17:384), on Isa 65:12.

divine calling, demands the engagement of the whole person. Luther continually warns that the preeminence of one station over another is reprehensible because it implies a contempt for the Creator. "We should remain there [in our vocation] with a happy conscience and know that through such work more is accomplished than if one had made donations to every monastery and received every medal; even if it is the most menial housework."[13] Thereby we are reminded of Luther's comment, "If everyone served their neighbor, then the whole world would be filled with divine service."[14]

Since a vocation should always be understood as God's calling and command, we are certain that our activity in this vocation is pleasing to God. When we are placed in a specific station, this means for us a certain challenge, and we should never be anxious that there is nothing for us to do. Since each vocation ultimately serves our neighbor, the right choice of profession loses its significance. Luther presupposes that somehow a calling is already waiting for us and we need not search for it through trials and tribulations.

Have we recognized that we are called (by God) to a certain service, then, we obtain the necessary professional certainty because as Christians we do not do anything without divine mandate, which means without calling. It is God's gift that we have a neighbor who is associated with us as a person, that we are allowed to live under a governing authority, and that we are tied into a family because on these points of contact to other people we are challenged to serve and to love. We can act here according to God's will and consider our work as divine service irrespective of its external, secular dimension.

Vocational Mobility

The question that must now be raised is whether placement within a particular vocation or station is inescapably fixed. Being tied to one

---

13 Martin Luther, *Predigten des Jahres 1529* (WA 29:566.39–567.20–21), sermon on Matt 9:1–3.

14 Martin Luther, *Predigten des Jahres 1544* (WA 49:606–14), sermon on Matt 22:34–36.

particular vocation or station is relativized by Luther since all people are of equal value before God. Nevertheless, he held firmly to the idea of unchangeable givens that place us within particular vocations. Hence he argues, for instance, that a woman cannot become a man, a pig herder cannot become a lawyer, and a peasant is not qualified to be mayor.[15] Biological and educational differences allocate us to specific vocations. We are not only born in a particular station but also placed in a particular vocation. Luther's view of stations and vocations remained within the framework of the societal structure of his time. He had to believe, therefore, that by birth people were called into particular stations.

But in many ways Luther also broke through the idea that society was structured according to the stations into which people were born. He fought, for example, against the practice of barring those born out of wedlock from holding honorable vocations within the craft and trade professions. They could only hold vocations that had no high esteem, such as barbers, executioners, or door-to-door salespersons. He also demanded the possibility for the advancement of children from parents of little income and schooling. But he did not thereby sanction the motive of increasing one's salary as justification for such advancement. Because every vocation is divine service, one cannot argue for a change in vocation on the basis of financial profit. Luther made parents vividly aware that through sufficient education, advancement to all government, educational, and ecclesiastical offices would be open to their children.

> It is not God's will that only those who are born kings, princes, lords, and nobles should exercise rule and lordship. He wills to have his beggars among them also, lest they think it is nobility of birth rather than God alone who makes lords and rulers. . . . That is the way it will always be: your son and my son, that is, the children of the common

---

15 See Luther, *Predigten des Jahres 1544* (WA 49:606–14), in sermon on Luke 14:1–3, where he emphasizes with many examples how one should not arrogantly seek to remove oneself from the station in which one has been placed.

people, will necessarily rule the world, both in the spiritual and the worldly estates.[16]

Advancement is open to all who have the prerequisite educational qualifications. Hence Luther impressed on the territorial lords the great importance of universities. He likewise wrote *To the Councilmen of All Cities in Germany That They Establish and Maintain Christian Schools*, as his writing of 1524 is titled. He demands that basic educational opportunities be available to all people. Hence the children of poor parents are to be supported through governmental and ecclesiastical scholarships. Yet all the different possibilities of advancement are of no use if parents do not allow their children in time to take advantage of available educational opportunities. Parents are also responsible for examining their children to determine whether they really have the necessary ability and interest to pursue higher education.

That one has had a good education, however, does not automatically mean that one should demand to take up a more highly qualified vocation than what one would have had without this education. As aforementioned, it does no damage to a craftsperson to have studied Latin just because it was an interesting subject, nor does it harm one to be well-educated, whether or not one actually takes up the kind of position normally associated with such studies.[17] For Luther there are no ethical value distinctions between the different vocations, and a fulfilling life is possible within each of them. If we are unable to achieve such career advancement, we should not consider ourselves deprived.

We can only choose our vocation within certain limits, for the calling to a vocation always takes place through other people. First we need a call, and then we can get active in this calling. Therefore, neither choosing a vocation nor the carrying out of its duties is a purely private matter. Luther frequently cautions parents and

16 Luther, *Sermon on Keeping Children in School* (*LW* 46:250–51).
17 Luther, *Sermon on Keeping Children in School* (*LW* 46:231–32).

teachers to keep in mind the well-being of the whole population when influencing a child regarding vocation. Important in regard to Luther's thoughts on vocation is a person's readiness to serve and to love.

> See to it first of all that you believe in Christ and are baptized. Afterward concern yourself with your vocation. I am called to be a pastor. Now when I preach I perform a holy work that is pleasing to God. If you are a father or mother, believe in Jesus Christ and so you will be a holy father and a holy mother. Take watch over the early years of your children, let them pray, and discipline, and spank them. Oversee the running of the household and the preparation of meals. Such things are nothing other than holy works for you have been called to do them. That means they are your holy life and are a part of God's Word and your calling.[18]

This mutual serving we encounter in the family and in marriage, as well as in the larger community, has already been shown to us in the service of Christ. We are called to serve each another, just as Christ served us.

Luther knew of no vocation that we could carry out without reference to the needs of the larger community. We are called when the community needs us for a specific service and when we are qualified to meet the demands of this service. We cannot derive from this calling either an inappropriate pride in our vocation or the absolute right of us as individuals to perform a particular vocation. A vocation is a service and can only be executed when both the necessary qualifications in those who would serve in this vocation and the need for it in the community are present. Under these conditions it is our duty not to forsake our vocation, even if it becomes too toilsome. If we have a genuine calling, then we dare not forsake our tasks but should stand courageously before them and accomplish them.

Luther's teaching on vocation can still in our own day help us to counter individualistic and self-centered striving for our own

---

18 Martin Luther, *Predigten des Jahres 1534* (*WA* 37:480.2–8), sermon on Luke 5:1–3.

advantage and to allow us to rediscover that our work is meant to serve the common good. We notice also in Luther's argumentation that the Christian faith is not simply an intellectual assent to certain principles but an active answer to God's summon that we care for the needs of our fellow human beings. But this chapter also shows us that five centuries separate us from Luther's time. The world has changed considerably since then. Yet many basic problems addressed by Luther have remained virtually the same.

Luther was the main representative of a conservative Reformation in contrast to the radicals, the Anabaptists or the social revolutionaries around Thomas Müntzer (1489–1525), and the spiritualists. Some of them wanted to change the world by force. But Luther does not advocate a restructuring of society and a change in the social structure of his time. He would even agree that a Christian government cannot solve all the social issues by its own power. Stemming from his conviction of the justification by faith alone, he had a deep distrust of all human endeavors to establish the kingdom of God on earth. In contrast to the Swiss reformers Zwingli and Calvin, he did not promulgate a new order of society.

But Luther also did not advocate a status quo by which he would have admonished his fellow Christians to suffer with humility and patience the then-existing conditions in society even when they were bad and unjust. We notice the opposite from his correspondence: he was deeply engaged in secular matters. For instance, he did not tolerate financial and societal egotism either for himself or for others. Without considering the personal consequences, he denounced both evildoers and their crimes and called for redress. But Luther left it up to secular institutions how to structure the living together of people. At the same time, he did not approve of their sins but reminded them of their obligation to a higher authority. His conviction that work performed in our world is not under ecclesial supervision, nor can it simply follow its own rules, but ultimately is under God's rule, can make us rediscover that work is neither an annoyance nor something that serves only ourselves. It is carried out to serve our fellow human beings.

This community aspect was rediscovered in many countries during the Covid-19 pandemic, when we suddenly realized how important is the work of cashiers in supermarkets, of nurses in hospitals and care facilities, and of garbage collectors in cities, to name just a few. Their services are often at the end of the salary scale but high up for the proper functioning of our society. That in some countries they were publicly thanked for their work is in Luther's view a contribution toward equalizing all services and vocations.

QUESTIONS FOR DISCUSSION

How is a vocation different from a job?
How is "station" different from social class?
Luther insisted that everyone has a vocation. How might we
    discern our vocations today?

CHAPTER NINE

Watching How People Speak

By now it has now become obvious that Luther was a multitalented person. During his stay at Wartburg, Luther translated the New Testament from Greek into German in just eleven weeks. It appeared in print in 1522 as the so-called *September Bible*. Prior to publication Philipp Melanchthon had reviewed the whole translation once more with Luther, since he was much better in Greek than Luther. Some other Wittenberg theologians also helped Luther with this edition, which appeared in three thousand copies and was sold out within three months, so that in December 1522 a second edition appeared. The New Testament was not cheap, as it cost half a guilder unbound, which corresponded to the weekly wage of a traveling carpenter. By 1534, the entire Bible was printed in German, and Luther worked throughout his life on improving its language. Until his death, the entire Bible translation or parts of it had been reissued more than four hundred times. As with all his publications, Luther did not receive a honorarium for his translation of the Bible. The profit remained with the printers.

Of course, there had been earlier translations of the Bible into German. But these translations were sometimes very rough and difficult to understand, since in Germany at Luther's time about twenty different languages or dialects were used, some of which differed considerably from each other. The language areas could be divided into Low German in the north and Upper German in the south. Since Luther had grown up in Eisleben, he knew Low German, and in Wittenberg, where he taught at the university, the common people spoke Low German. The electoral administration and the university made more use of High German, which absorbed southern German influences. Luther used both Low German and Upper German elements in his translation of the Bible. Basically, it was the Saxon chancellery language, which could be understood in both Low German and Upper German areas and which Luther molded into a lively and expressive language without the stilted style of an electoral chancellery. Thanks to the wide distribution of his Bible, this language finally prevailed and thus played a decisive role in the development of a uniform, dialect-free German language.

As far as we know, Luther's translation of the Bible, or at least part of it, was soon available in every fifth household in the German-speaking areas. Although only a few could read at that time, the whole household community probably gathered in the evening, and those who were knowledgeable about reading read from the Luther Bible. So, the Bible or parts of the Bible were for many the only printed texts that were read at that time. Since Luther's translation of the Bible had such a great influence, it is not surprising that the Council of Trent (1545–1563) placed it on the index of forbidden books.

1. LUTHER AS A CREATOR OF LANGUAGE

Journalist Christian Feldmann wrote of Martin Luther in the *Frankfurter Allgemeine Zeitung* in 2017, perhaps a little exaggerated but not without reason, that he was "the most ingenious language creator of all time."[1] Luther used many words in his translation work that were understandable beyond the boundaries of dialect, and he also coined many new words and terms, such as "peaceful" (*friedfertig*),

---

1 Christian Feldmann, "Der genialste Sprachschöpfer aller Zeiten," *Frankfurter Allgemeine Zeitung*, June 12, 2017, https://tinyurl.com/hnnw57av.

"power word" (*Machtwort*), "zeal of fire" (*Feuereifer*), or "gap filler" (*Lückenbüßer*). Expressive phrases, such as "the hair of my flesh bristled" (*mir standen die Haare zu Berge*; Job 4:15) or "who built his house on sand" (*sein Haus auf Sand bauen*; Matt 7:26), he created for his translation of the Bible. He also adopted proverbs from the vernacular to use for his translation, such as "pride goes before destruction" (*Hochmut kommt vor dem Fall*; Prov 16:18) and "justice will return to the righteous" (*Recht muss Recht bleiben*; Ps 94:15).

Luther listened closely to how the people around him spoke and often struggled for every expression and word for several weeks. He writes: "I have been diligent in interpreting that I want to render in pure and clear German. And we have encountered very often that we have searched and asked for a single word for fourteen days, three, four weeks, but sometimes we have not found it. So at Job we, Magister Philip, Aurogallus and I, worked that we could sometimes hardly cover three lines in four days."[2] Although Luther often used a very hearty way of expression, which was not unusual in the time of Grobianism, he almost completely dispensed with such expressions in his translation of the Bible. He thus used an upscale but by no means artificial language.[3]

Eight years after the *September Bible*, Luther wrote in 1530 a *Letter about Translating* (*Sendbrief vom Dolmetschen*), in which he explains what is important to him in his translation work. For Luther, Latin, the colloquial language of scholars at the time, was a matter of course. But that wasn't true for the average person. That is why he writes in this letter: "You don't have to ask the letters in the Latin language how to talk German . . . , but you have to ask the mother in the house, the children in the alleys, the common man in the market and look

---

2 Martin Luther, *Sendbrief vom Dolmetschen* (1530; WA 30/II:636.15–20). Aurogallus, actually Matthäus Goldhahn, was professor of Greek, Latin, and Hebrew in Wittenberg since 1519.

3 Luther even influenced how people wrote. In his translation of the Bible in 1534, for example, he was the first to capitalize nouns almost throughout. In the seventeenth century, this regulation disappeared in all European languages except in German. Here, too, Germans still follow Luther's example.

at the same persons at their mouth, how they talk, and translate accordingly; that's when they understand it and realize that you are talking to them in German."[4]

For Luther, it was therefore important not simply to translate from one language to another but also to ask whether the reader understood what had been translated. As an example, he quotes in Latin the saying of Christ *Ex abundantia cordis os loquitur*, which could be translated, "From the abundance of the heart speaks the mouth."[5] But Luther objects, "What German would understand such a thing?" That is why he translates, "Of whom the heart is full, the mouth speaks" (*Wes das Herz voll ist, des gehet der Mund über*), because that's how the mother in the house and the common man spoke. Even more blatant is the following example, which Luther cites from Mark 14:4: *Ut quid perditio ista unguenti facta est?*[6] Literally, one could translate this, "Why did this loss of the ointments happen?" But Luther rightly asks what kind of German this is. He, on the other hand, translates, "What's such a pity? No, it's a pity about the ointment" (*Was soll solcher Schade? Nein, es ist schade um die Salbe*). "This is good German from which one understands that Magdalena handled the spilled ointment inappropriately and wasted it."

On the one hand, Luther wanted to translate as accurately as possible, but not so literally in the literary sense that no one understood the text. On the other hand, the translation should be as free as necessary, with the average person, whether man or woman, being his authoritative guarantor. Only if they understood the text was the translation successful. For example, he translates the angel's address to Mary, "Greetings, favored one!" (*du holdselige Maria*) and not "Thou full of grace, Mary" (*du voll von Gnaden Maria*), because Mary is not a barrel of beer or a bag full of money.[7] According to Luther, every German can imagine what the angel means. Of

---

4 Luther, *Sendbrief vom Dolmetschen* (WA 30/II:637.17–22).
5 Luther, *Sendbrief vom Dolmetschen* (WA 30/II:637.23.26.32).
6 Luther, *Sendbrief vom Dolmetschen* (WA 30/II:637.36–7.38–9; 638.8–9).
7 Luther, *Sendbrief vom Dolmetschen* (WA 30/II:638.13–27).

course, the language has changed in the meantime, and *holdselig* is no longer understandable for everyone. For Luther, it was crucial that every layperson could read and understand God's word without official mediators and translation aids, which were hard to find. This broke the clergy's monopoly on interpretation, and everyone could understand God's word for themselves.

In the case of important biblical passages, according to Luther, he did not deviate very freely from the text, but "where it mattered, I kept it after the letters and did not deviate so freely from it."[8] As an example, he refers to John 6:27, where Christ says, "God the Father has set his seal" (*Diesen hat Gott der Vater versiegelt*). Although it would have been better German to write, "This one was marked by God the Father" (*Diesen hat Gott der Vater gezeichnet*), or, "This is the one whom the Father means" (*Diesen meinet der Vater*), Luther nevertheless kept a more literal and precise translation, so that the meaning is preserved as accurately as possible, even if the alternatives would have been more understandable. It is not surprising that Luther emphasizes that not everyone understands how to translate. Not only does one have to be pious and faithful, but one also has to have a large vocabulary at one's disposal so that one can use the right words in each case.

2. UNDERSTANDING THE MEANING
OF THE BIBLICAL TEXT

After Luther reworked the Psalms in German translation with his collaborators, he wrote a short pamphlet on translating, because the Psalms offered him enough examples of his approach.[9] In it he explains the principles according to which he translates:

---

8 Luther, *Sendbrief vom Dolmetschen* (WA 30/II:640.20–22).

9 Martin Luther, *Summarien über die Psalmen und die Ursachen des Dolmetschen* (1531–1533; WA 38:9–18).

Whether we sometimes depart from the Grammaticis and Rabbinis here, and the like, shall no one be surprised; for we have kept the rule: where the words may allow it, and give a better understanding, we have not allowed ourselves to be forced by the grammars made by rabbis to the lesser or different understanding; how all schoolmasters teach that it is not the meaning that serves and follows the words, but the words that serve and follow the meaning.[10]

Especially with the Psalms, which were often written in verse form, it is important, according to Luther, to first grasp the right meaning. Then one has to express this meaning in words that are understandable in German, instead of sticking literally to words that only roughly express the meaning and are often incomprehensible. That is why Luther emphasizes:

Whoever wants to speak German does not have to use the way of the Hebrew words, but must see to it, if he understands the Hebrew man, that he grasps the meaning and thinks like this: Dear, how does the German man speak in such a case? If he now has the German words that serve this purpose, let the Hebrew words go, and freely speak out the meaning in the best possible German, as he can.[11]

Luther illustrates this in Psalm 68:14, which literally says in Hebrew, "As you will lie between the marks, the wings of the doves are covered with silver, and their wings are covered with glistening gold" (*So ihr zwischen den Marken liegen werdet, so sind die Flügel der Tauben mit Silber überzogen und ihre Fittiche mit gleißendem Gold*). Luther rightly argues that hardly anyone would understand such German and then translates, "The wings of a dove covered with silver, its pinions with green gold" (*Die Flügel der Tauben sind überzogen mit Silber, und ihre Schwingen schimmern von Gold*; Ps 68:13). The intention of the text is thus met, even if it is not a literal translation.

---

10 Luther, *Summarien über die Psalmen* (WA 38:11.11–17).
11 Luther, *Summarien über die Psalmen* (WA 38:11.27–32).

Sometimes Luther's translation is tantamount to an interpretation. Psalm 118:27 literally says, "Bind the festal procession with branches, up to the horns of the altar" (*Bindet das Opfer mit Seilen, bis an die Hörner des Altars*). By the sacrifice (of the festal procession), the psalmist means the Passover or Easter lamb, which is to be led to the altar with ropes and eaten at home after its sacrificial death. Luther, however, points the whole thing to Christ, which is why we should praise God, and translates quite freely, "Decorate the feast with *Maien* to the horns of the altar" (*Schmücket das Fest mit Maien bis an die Hörner des Altars*). The term *Maien* originally referred to a branch standing in juice, a term that is no longer easily understood today. The present-day German translation of the Bible according to Luther has retained this expression, while the joint translation of the Catholic and Protestant Churches in Germany offers a now more comprehensible translation: "Dance the feast with branches up to the horns of the altar!" (*Tanzt den Festreigen mit Zweigen bis zu den Hörnern des Altars*). This is entirely in Luther's spirit, as he writes: "We have indeed spared no diligence or effort. Who can do it better, to whom we grant it."[12]

Luther and his collaborators put a lot of effort into working out a Bible translation for Christians that was generally understandable. However, since language is constantly changing, this translation has had to be revised to this day. Without it being his intention, Luther's translation of the Bible made a significant contribution to the development of the New High German language, which he also enriched with many terms and proverbs still used today. Feldmann sums up:

Among those who have gradually replaced the chaos of the countless dialects [in Germany] with a supra-regional, generally understandable language, he [Luther] is undoubtedly the most influential and effective, the most talented and original. In other countries, a uniform language was formed in the metropolises and at the princely courts, or it was decreed by political power. In Germany, it [the German language] paved the way for itself with a literary text that everyone knew and

---

12 Luther, *Summarien über die Psalmen* (WA 38:16.17–19).

many loved: with the national appropriation of the Bible in the translation of Martin Luther.[13]

QUESTIONS FOR DISCUSSION

What was Luther's philosophy of translation?
How did his translation of the Bible influence the German language?

---

13 Feldmann, "Der genialste Sprachschöpfer aller Zeiten."

CHAPTER TEN

Against Predatory Capitalism

We have noticed that Martin Luther was much more than just a reformer of the church. He had become such a public figure that there was hardly any issue in the church or public life on which his opinion or advice was not sought. This held also true for economic matters, in which Luther certainly was not an expert. In contrast to his wife, Katy, who had to run a large household with male and female helpers plus students who lived as boarders in their house, Luther was personally indifferent to money and wealth. It was only important for him that Katy was financially afloat and had something left for those in need. Yet with an open mind and well-versed in Scripture, Luther could distinguish between right and wrong even in economic matters.

During Luther's time, 90 percent of the population in the Germany lived in the countryside, and therefore the majority of the people were peasants. Nearly half of them did not own any property and were dependent on the goodwill of various landlords, such as the nobility, monasteries, or prosperous citizens. Even in smaller cities such as Wittenberg, with roughly two thousand inhabitants, many of the citizens were still active in farming, as we can see from Luther's own wife, Katy. She supported her family from the land she was cultivating and from the chickens and pigs she raised. At the same time commerce was flourishing, especially in rich merchant cities such as

Augsburg and Nuremberg. The discovery of the Americas opened new dimensions for commerce from South America to India and from the Baltic Sea to Spain. Revenues for a few merchants increased in an unprecedented way. Jacob Fugger the Rich (1459–1525) from Augsburg, for instance, was so rich he could advance money not only to the archbishop Albrecht of Mainz but also to the emperor.[1] At the same time, the price of manufactured goods increased considerably, so that many craftsmen and artisans advanced to entrepreneurship while their helpers received only a tiny share of the revenues. For instance, Lucas Cranach the Elder (1472–1553) was not only a famous painter but also owned a pharmacy and a printing press—he printed Luther's *September Bible*—and had a monopoly of the sale on medicines in Wittenberg, and until 1545 he held several times the office of mayor in Wittenberg. Similarly, Albrecht Dürer (1471–1528) not only sold his paintings in his hometown of Nuremberg but made agreements with agents to sell his "copper and wood etchings from one country to another and from one town to another" for the highest price possible.[2] With the rise of this new capitalism, the gap between the rich and the poor or the nearly poor widened more and more. This did not pass unnoticed for Luther, since he also came from a family that had been on the rise to prosperity through involvement in the copper mining business.

Once Luther got married in 1525, he was exposed to the daily economic problems in Wittenberg by feeding his own family. His wife was astute in financing the household by having student boarders, buying a small farm near her ancestral home in Zölsdorf, and being

---

1 According to Martin Brecht, *Martin Luther: His Road to the Reformation, 1483–1521*, trans. James Schaaf (Philadelphia: Fortress, 1985), 179, the Fugger banking house made a profit of 52,286 ducats on the sum of 21,000 ducats, which it advanced to the archbishop. This was a profit or more than 200 percent! Luther rightly wonders, "How could it ever be right and according to God's will that a man in such a short time should grow so rich that he could buy out kings and emperors?" Martin Luther, *Trade and Usury* (1524; *LW* 45:271). See also the explanatory footnote on the same page.

2 Ludwig Veit, "Albrecht Dürer und seine Familie: Dokumente," in *Albrecht Dürer 1471–1971*, 3rd ed. (Munich: Prestel, 1971), 31, 43.

nearly self-sufficient in terms of food. Yet Luther noticed the high interest rates that were being charged and occasionally complained about the high food prices even if there was a good harvest.[3] It is no surprise that soon Luther addressed economic issues more specifically. Already in his 1520 publication *To the Christian Nobility* he labeled luxurious clothing, exotic spices, and buying on credit as sources for sliding into poverty.[4] He also wondered how the Fuggers and others could amass so much wealth.

Charging interest was debated among Christians from early on, since with reference to passages such as Exodus 22:25 ("If you lend money to my people, to the poor among you, you shall not deal with them as a creditor; you shall not exact interest from them"), it was inferred that Christians should not lend money for financial gain. Christian should simply help each other when they were in need. Perhaps this was too idealistic, and therefore Pope Leo the Great (ca. 400–461) prohibited both clerics and laypeople from "lay[ing] out money at interest, and wish[ing] to enrich themselves as usurers."[5] Several church councils reiterated this prohibition. Yet Thomas Aquinas (ca. 1225–1274) and other scholastic theologians thought it legitimate to ask for interest if a person did not pay back the loan in time or if the one who loaned money could not get back all or part of the loan, or for someone to pay interest out of gratitude.[6] This means that taking interest was not totally illegitimate.

In 1500 an imperial diet at Augsburg decided that *Zinsskauf*—literally meaning "interest purchase"—was legal.[7] In order to avoid paying interest on a loan, which was forbidden by the church as usury, the moneylender now gave a certain amount of money to a

3 See Martin Brecht, *Martin Luther: Shaping and Defining the Reformation, 1521–1532*, trans. James Schaaf (Philadelphia: Fortress, 1990), 145.

4 See Luther, *To the Christian Nobility* (*LW* 44:212–13).

5 Leo the Great, *Letter* 4.3, in *NPNF²* 12:3–4.

6 See Thomas Aquinas, *Summa theologica*, II–II, question 78 ("The Sin of Usury"), answer 2, response.

7 According to Hans-Jürgen Prien, *Luthers Wirtschaftsethik* (Göttingen: Vandenhoeck & Ruprecht, 1992), 63.

person and in return "bought" a regular *zinss* or income from this credit. This could be done in various ways: (1) One could borrow money, and the one who advanced the money would then obtain a specified piece of land of the borrower's property as a security. (2) The one who advanced the money would receive a portion of the harvest determined in advance. (3) The whole property and not just a piece of the land could be obtained as a security, a deal called *blind Zinsskauf.*

The problem Luther saw in the *Zinsskauf* was that the one who advanced the money had virtually no risk. The debtor had to pay a certain fixed portion either in money or in goods from the land on which the money was given, regardless whether it was a good year or a bad one. So if the yield on the land was bad, the debtor still had to fulfill the stipulation of the deal. If the security for the loan was not just a certain piece of land but the whole property of the debtor, then the whole property could be lost if things went bad for the borrower. The issue of the *Zinsskauf* shows that the prohibition against charging interest had many loopholes for Christians. In the case of Jews this was even more so, because they were virtually pushed into the money business.

In canon 25 of the Third Lateran Council (1179) the laws against usury were increased in severity, and Christian burial was refused to those who had sinned against this prohibition. When Christians shied away from taking interest, the business of moneylending came more and more into the hands of the Jews. The reason for this was that in many countries Jews were not allowed to be involved in craftsmanship and other honorable businesses, and in some countries they could not even own property. Therefore the moneylending business was often the main enterprise in which they could be engaged. Many small businesses needed more money than they had, and here it was the Jews who came to help. But in times of economic crises, Jews were often called usurers and even expelled from cities so that indebted persons could get rid of their debts. In the Middle Ages, then, a kind of anti-Judaism evolved, and the Jews were stereotyped as rich, avaricious, and fraudulent.

It is not surprising that Luther as a child of his time also lambasted Jews. Indeed, two editions of his *Sermon against Usury* of 1519 showed a Jew on the cover with the words "pay or give interest," while the third depicted only a teacher with four persons intently listening, two of them being Jews.[8] The same is true of three printings of his second sermon on this topic of 1520, while the other nine printings are without such caricatures. Luther excused himself by saying that he was unable to also take care of the illustrations of his publications. But since they were originally printed in Wittenberg, Luther could have avoided such caricatures if he really wanted to do so. His later publications against usury do not show such caricatures, even if his attitude toward the Jews and their moneylending business reflects popular opinion among the people prevalent at that time.[9] But what did Luther actually write?

1. LUTHER'S *SMALL SERMON ON USURY* (1519/20)

Around the turn of sixteenth century, there was an unusually high number of bad harvests, such as in 1490–1494, 1500–1504, and 1515–1519. This caused many peasants to take out loans that they could not pay back, and therefore they were forced to lose their property. Luther then wrote a *Small Sermon on Usury* in 1519, in which he states with reference to the Old Testament that one should willingly and with a glad heart loan money to someone who is in need without any interest (Deut 15:7–11). Nobody should have to beg or go hungry. Pointing to Luke 6:30–35, Luther writes, "From these words it becomes evident that a Christian should freely give and loan and moreover should be nice to his enemies and neither quarrel with them or harm them."[10]

---

8 See Luther, *(Kleiner) Sermon von dem Wucher* (1519; WA 6:2).

9 See his publications *Trade and Usury* (1524; LW 45:245–73) and *An die Pfarrherrn wider den Wucher zu predigen, Vermahnung* (1540; WA 52:327–28), and for the whole issue of Luther and the Jews on economic matters, see Prien, *Luthers Wirtschaftsethik*, 69–71.

10 Luther, *(Kleiner) Sermon von dem Wucher* (WA 6:4.36–5.2).

If we loan out to others wine, grain, money, or whatever and level on them so much interest that they must pay back more than they have borrowed, this is "a Jewish ploy and it is an un-Christian procedure since it goes against the holy Gospel of Christ, nay even against the natural law." Luther refers here to the golden rule in Luke 6:31 ("Do to others as you would have them do to you"). Nobody likes to pay interest. So why demand it from others? Luther realizes that this is not a welcome advice and therefore simply says, "If you do not do it, then you are also not a Christian and you will have received your heaven here on earth." He sums up his advice: "Christian business and benevolence with temporal goods consists of three points: give without charge, loan without interest, and let it go with love."[11]

It was different with the so-called *Zinsskauf*. Luther agrees that in this case one can charge 4, 5, or 6 percent depending how good the yield of a field is against which the interest is charged. Yet to charge 7 to 10 percent is usury and robbery, because "here the poor common people are stealthily drained dry and heavily oppressed."[12] Even in money matters one should always serve the neighbor without doing the neighbor any harm. He still thought that this *Zinsskauf* was somewhat questionable, since the interest was safe but one never knew how the harvest would do. So the one who advanced the money could lean back, while the other party bore all the risk. Already two months later, in December 1519, Luther considerably expanded his sermon into the *Long Sermon on Usury*. Evidently his publication had been met with some resistance and therefore he wanted to explain in detail his position "so that Christ's pure doctrine should not cause even more offense."[13]

For Luther, it is very important that financial transactions be conducted without force or violence. He refers here to Matthew 5:40: "If anyone wants to sue you and take your coat, give your cloak as

---

11 Luther, *(Kleiner) Sermon von dem Wucher* (WA 6:6.6–8, 19–20, 12–14).

12 See Luther, *(Kleiner) Sermon von dem Wucher* (WA 6:6.24–40).

13 According to the introduction of the *Long Sermon on Usury* (1520; WA 6:33). This quote is not in the English translation.

well." While some things are not punishable in the court, such as self-defense or quarreling, such is not deemed good by God. "Now for everyone to demand what is his and be unwilling to endure wrong is not the way to peace."[14] If one pushes through one's right with every means, the gain is often less than the investment in the cause. We should always attempt to settle financial matters in a peaceful manner.

Then Luther picks up his second point: "that we are to give freely and without return to anyone who needs our goods or asks for them."[15] Again he refers to a biblical precept: "Give to everyone who begs from you, and do not refuse anyone who wants to borrow from you" (Matt 5:42). Luther distinguishes between lending and giving, saying that lending means that one will get it back sooner or later but without something in addition, meaning interest, while giving means that one does not expect a return of the given item. Moreover, in Christianity nobody should need to beg or go hungry. The open hand should be extended not only to one's friends but even to one's enemies and opponents. Then Luther cautions that one should not just give to the church, especially for building St. Peter's basilica in Rome, because one thinks that this is an especially good deed. Luther does not want to "disallow the building of suitable churches and their adornment; we cannot do without them. Any public worship ought rightly to be conducted in the finest way. But there should be a limit to this, and we should take care that the appurtenances of worship be pure, rather than costly." The main stream of benevolence should flow toward the poor and needy, that these deeds "would shine more brightly than all churches of wood and stone."[16] Each town and village should build and furnish its own churches, and also make provision itself to care for its poor so that beggars no longer need to move from place to place.

14 Luther, *Long Sermon on Usury* (LW 45:273, 279).
15 Luther, *Long Sermon on Usury* (LW 45:280).
16 Luther, *Long Sermon on Usury* (LW 45:285–86).

Having summed up his main points—we should give without wanting the given item returned to us, we should lend items without asking more in return than we have lent, and we should let things go in peace if they are taken from us by force—he now turns to the novel item *Zinsskauf*. Luther cautions, "Although the *zinss* contract is now established as a proper and admissible operation, it is nevertheless an odious and hateful practice for many reasons."[17] The one who advances money is always better off than the one who receives it.[18]

In order to have the risk not just on the side of the one who receives the needed money, Luther states that the debtor should not be liable with his whole property, but just with part of it, so that the debtor does not drift into poverty by losing his whole property if he cannot pay the *zinss*. The risk should not just rest with the debtor but also with the one who loans the money since he does not really do anything with his money, while the debtor does. Only the debtor should be allowed to call in the advanced money, but not the one who advanced it, since this could again lead to poverty. Yet if the debtor has done wrong with the money he may be liable to the one who advanced the money for the lost profit from the deal.

Small wonder that Luther called these loan sharks "usurer, thieves, and robbers, for they are selling the money's luck, which is not theirs or within their power."[19] Too easily and too quickly a debtor could end up in poverty without it being the debtor's own fault. Luther stipulates that the debtor need not pay the interest until the debtor can undertake his labor free, healthy, and without problems. This means if the debtor works on his property but it does not yield what was expected in a way that is not his own fault, he does not owe anything to the person who advanced the loan. "If you want to have an interest in my profits you must also have an interest in my losses,"

---

17 Luther, *Long Sermon on Usury* (*LW* 45:295–96).

18 See on the following the excellent contribution by Andreas Pawlas, "Luther zu Geld und Zins. Mit einem Vorwort über Lutherische Erwägungen zu Geld und Zins," University of Uppsala, Working Paper 2013, 28, https://tinyurl.com/2mcwxxbn.

19 Luther, *Long Sermon on Usury* (*LW* 45:301–2).

the debtor should say to the buyer, according to Luther.[20] If there is no shared risk, there is usury, according to Luther. For him the best solution would be to follow the biblical command of tithing, which in the case of need could be lowered to the ninth, or eighth, or sixth portion.

> Then everything would be perfectly consistent, and all would depend on the grace and blessing of God. If the tithe turned out well in any year, it would bring the recipient of *zinss* a good sum; if it turned out badly, it would bring in but little. The creditor would thus have to bear both risk and good fortune as well as the debtor, and both of them would have to look for God. . . .The tithe is, therefore, the best *zinss* of all. It has been in use since the beginning of the world, and in the Old Law is praised and confirmed as the fairest of all arrangements according to divine and natural law.[21]

Luther is no biblicist but appeals both to the biblical precedent and to reason. He is also open to more or less than one-tenth of the yield depending on the circumstances. But he does not want a fixed amount of money to be the same every year, since that amount could quickly drive many debtors into poverty. The nobility should supervise such suggestions, and an imperial diet should decide on appropriate laws so that usury would be curbed.

2. *TRADE AND USURY* (1524)

Just a few years later Luther had to deal again with the issue of taking interest when Dr. Jacob Strauss (ca. 1480–ca. 1532) arrived in Wittenberg in 1522 and was called to be pastor at St. George in Eisenach the following year. There Strauss published a collection of articles in which he claimed that not only charging interest but also paying it was a sin, since whoever pays interest is an accomplice in usury. As a Christian the debtor must be more obedient to God than to the one

---

20 Luther, *Long Sermon on Usury* (*LW* 45303).
21 Luther, *Long Sermon on Usury* (*LW* 45309).

who loaned money, because the Bible says one should loan but not take anything in return. As expected, some debtors no longer paid interest, which hurt especially church institutions that depended on this kind of income.

Luther was asked to write an opinion on behalf of John Frederick the Magnanimous (1503–1554), the son of Duke John the Steadfast of Saxony (1468–1532), who was instrumental in church politics. On October 18, 1523, he wrote a memorandum to Saxon chancellor Georg von Brück (1484–1557). There Luther points out that the most dangerous point in the pamphlet of Strauss is his teaching

> that the debtor ought not pay the interest to the usurious creditor for then he would be agreeing with the usurious creditor and would sin with him. This is not right. Because the debtor has acted correctly and is free of sin, if he tells the creditor that [the business transaction] is usury and points out its iniquity. Yet the debtor should not take revenge, but should consent to pay the unjust creditor.[22]

While Luther agrees with Strauss that lending money at interest is unchristian, he is realistic that it can never be curbed completely and turned into a decent system, "since all the world is greedy."

Luther then elaborated the issues involved in moneylending and commerce more extensively in his writing of 1524, *Trade and Usury*, but he had no illusion that his opinion would be heeded by all. But he realized that people who knew the gospel could judge by their conscience what was appropriate and what was not. Therefore he turned to those who would rather be poor with God than rich with the devil. While it is clear that buying and selling is necessary, he wonders whether all luxury items are needed or whether they just drain money and funnel it to other countries. Luther does not approve of the idea of selling goods as expensively as possible without regard for the buyer, since thereby one sins against the neighbor. One robs and steals the neighbor's means. The rule of the merchants should

---

22 Martin Luther, "To Gregory Brück," October 18, 1523 (*LW* 49:52–54 [letter 136]). The issue was here whether social laws of the Old Testament such as Deut 15:1–11 had to be kept by the Christian community.

not be, "I may sell my wares as dear as I can and will; but I may sell my wares as dear as I ought, or as it is right and fair."[23] The merchant has a responsibility to God and the neighbor. There is no fixed profit, because the price depends on one's own cost, the investment, and the danger incurred in procuring the goods. This was to be especially considered when the wares were from distant countries. The roads were not safe because they were lacking maintenance, and there were also robbers, who endangered commerce. Yet "laborers deserve their food" (Matt 10:10) is Luther's advice, and if one takes too much profit, one must pray, "Forgive us our debts," since no person's life is without sin.

In a second part Luther deals with the issue of becoming surety for another. He very bluntly calls this "a foolish thing to do."[24] Scripture tells us that we should trust God alone and not humans. "For human nature is false, vain, deceitful, and unreliable, as Scripture says and experience daily teaches."[25] By extending insurance, one trusts a person and endangers one's life and property. Since this is not a good option, what else should one do? Among Christians, Luther says, we should give away our property and take it back again if it is returned to us. But if it is not returned, we must do without it. We should lend freely and take our chances on getting it back. Christians are brothers and sisters, "and one does not forsake another; neither is any of them so lazy and shameless that he would not work but depend simply on another's wealth and labor." Where there are no Christians, Luther charges the secular authorities with seeking to return what has been borrowed. If they "will not help him to recover his loan, let him lose it."[26] "Since Christians are a rare minority on earth, the authorities ought to compel those who are not Christians

---

23 Luther, *Trade and Usury* (*LW* 45:248).

24 Luther, *Trade and Usury* (*LW* 45:253). To minimize risks in commerce, the idea evolved that for a fee an owner transferred the risks of his property to an insurer. When the goods were lost, this could become a costly issue for the insurer.

25 Luther, *Trade and Usury* (*LW* 45:253).

26 Luther, *Trade and Usury* (*LW* 45:258, 260).

to repay what they have borrowed. Luther also stipulates that one is not obligated to make a loan except out of one's surplus and what one can spare from one's own needs. Our first and greatest obligation is to our own dependents.

He deals extensively with the threat that emerges if one or a few merchants gain a monopoly on certain items, especially if they are imported from far away. They sell them as dear as they like, or only see the neighbors' need and do not relieve it but make the most of it and get rich at the neighbors' expense. "All such fellows are manifest thieves, robbers, and usurers."[27] He calls again on secular authorities to thwart such misuse of power. "The temporal authorities would do right if they took from such fellows everything they had, and drove them out of the country."[28] People such as these are not worthy to be called human beings and should not to be allowed to live among us.

Luther then shows by examples how the prices of goods were raised to exorbitant heights. It is the duty of the princes "to use their duly constituted authority in punishing the injustices of the merchants and preventing them from so shamefully skinning their subjects." Yet he surmises that the princes are in cohorts with the merchants. He is convinced, however, that injustice will not be left unpunished by God. God "uses one rascal to flog the other."[29]

3. EXHORTATION TO THE CLERGY TO PREACH AGAINST EXPLOITATIVE INTEREST (1540)

Since usury had become rampant, Luther thought he should take up his pen again. He asks all the preachers not to desist from preaching against usury and to admonish and warn the people. He follows the decisions of the church and writes, "If you advance money and ask or take more for it than you initially gave, it is usury and rightly

---

27 Luther, *Trade and Usury* (LW 45:262).
28 Luther, *Trade and Usury* (LW 45:265).
29 Luther, *Trade and Usury* (LW 45:270).

condemned.[30] A charge of 5 or 6 percent interest is already usury. He is not talking about giving or selling but loaning. According to him, we should expect that we receive back only that which we have loaned and not more. If one would object that then nobody would loan anything, Luther retorts that loaning without charge is "a good work," because nobody else does it.[31] It serves those who are in need.

Luther realizes that this is a worldly or secular issue, the resolution of which the preacher can contribute little. It is rather a case for the lawyers, who must prohibit usury, and when it occurs it should be punished. Among many other historical examples, Luther refers to Aristotle, who wrote that the most hated sort of getting rich is usury. It "makes a gain out of money itself, and not from the natural object of it. For money was intended to be used in exchange, but not to increase at interest. And this term interest, which means the birth of money from money, is applied to the breeding of money because the offspring resembles the parent. Wherefore of any modes of getting wealth this is the most unnatural."[32] For Luther, Aristotle was still an authority in secular matters. Luther followed him and argued against usury on account of natural reason. He cites with disdain that in cities such as Leipzig, lenders charged more than 40 percent interest so that by paying interest a citizen or a peasant would be devoured within a year.[33] He says that lawyers and princes must join together so that this thievery ceases. He ends this chapter by asserting once more that good works are "giving, loaning, and suffering."[34] Christians can have no part in usury.

In the next chapter Luther talks about giving and, referring to Matthew 5:42, "Give to everyone," he explains that this means we should give to everybody who is in need, both friends and foes. This does not include those, however, who do not want to work or

---

30 Martin Luther, *An die Pfarrherrn wider den Wucher zu predigen, Vermahnung* (1540; WA 51:332.32–33).

31 Luther, *An die Pfarrherrn* (WA 51:337.32).

32 Aristotle, *Pol.* 1.10, trans. Benjamin Jowett, https://tinyurl.com/47yn72h4.

33 See Luther, *An die Pfarrherrn* (WA 51:365.18–19).

34 Luther, *An die Pfarrherrn* (WA 51:380.23).

who are not from your city.[35] It also does not mean giving if you do not have what you yourself need, nor does it mean to give away everything, because then you could not give anything tomorrow if need arises. Freely giving should not imply that one then becomes a beggar. Giving also should not be done so that one reaps benefits from it or is celebrated for this deed. Luther would abhor the contemporary idea, "Do something good and speak about it." No, he says, with reference to Romans 12:8 ("the giver, in generosity"), just do it and then forget it "as if you had never given anything or done something charitable."[36]

Luther then talks about loaning. Again, this covers both friends and foes, and is extended to those in need. The maxim that provides guidance here is the golden rule: do as you expect to have done to you. We should not rejoice in the misery of a person but be merciful, with an open hand. "There is no greater enemy of humans—except for the devil—than a greedy person and a usurer, because such a person wants to be god over all people."[37] That Luther lashes out so much against such people shows the rampant problems he encountered: in order to get rich as quickly as possible, people had no concern for the well-being of others. Here Christian love was wanting. As Luther writes, worldly authority was either too weak or too unconcerned to take redeeming action. In part, this authority was an accomplice, living in splendor at the expense of its subjects.

Then Luther comes to his third and final point, which he had already mentioned in his earlier writings: Christians should be willing to suffer. They should not take justice into their own hands. They will find many who make people suffer among the secular authorities in the city halls, among the citizens and the nobility, since they neither give nor loan and help. Even pastors suffer as a result of these people, since pastors are only guests in the parsonage and once they

---

35 At that time there were many beggars who went from one city to another to beg.

36 Luther, *An die Pfarrherrn* (WA 51:387.19–20).

37 Luther, *An die Pfarrherrn* (WA 51:396.28–30).

die their widows often become beggars. Luther learned through visitations that started in Electoral Saxony in 1525 that often parsonages looked like dumps. Yet he does not close on a downcast note. Even if there is suffering, one should not despair. "Just be a pious Christian, preacher, pastor, citizen, peasant, nobleperson, lord, and conduct your office diligently and trustworthy. . . . Just be a true Christian who suffers with a simple heart for God's sake and does not give cause for suffering."[38] But Luther also ends with tongue in cheek: the greedy people and the usurers should not think that he is totally against them, since there is a rich Lord who will play along with them, and he will return to them a hundred- and a thousandfold, namely, God, the Creator of heaven and earth. "He had offered us through his dear son in the Gospel: 'Give and loan, then it shall be returned to you' not just the same but much more, namely a good measure, a measure shaken together, a measure pressed down, a measure running over."[39] Here would be the right place to exercise usury. The problem, Luther concedes, is that people will not heed this advice.

4. LUTHER'S CHALLENGE TO ECONOMIC PRAXIS

When one reads his four publications on usury, one realizes that over the years Luther's line of argumentation has hardly changed. At the most one could say that his tone became harsher, and there was reason for this, since in spring of 1539 food became exorbitantly expensive in the Wittenberg area on account of little rain during the preceding summer and an artificial shortage to obtain even higher prices.[40] Many people were starving, and small merchants heaped more and more debts on their possessions or were even driven out of existence. Luther interceded with the mayor of Wittenberg, Lukas

---

38 Luther, *An die Pfarrherrn* (WA 51:412.23–25, 30–32).
39 Luther, *An die Pfarrherrn* (WA 51:419.24–27).
40 For the following, see Theodor Strohm, "Luthers Wirtschafts- und Sozialethik," in Junghans, *Leben und Werk Martin Luthers* 1:215–17.

Cranach the Elder, and also with the elector John Frederick. He tried to address the evil with theological arguments. In agreement with the Sermon on the Mount, Christians should not renege on paying the due interest and trust God that God will give them their daily bread. They also should give everyone without asking for a financial return. In rejecting the notion of asking for interest payments, he was in agreement with the Fifth Lateran Council of 1515, which had renewed the prohibition on charging interest. But in reality there were many exceptions.[41]

In his appeal to the magistrates and the nobility, Luther asked that interest rates be charged in accordance with laws and customs in an appropriate way. This meant that the interest rate should not been higher than 5 percent and should be reduced if the yield that was achieved with the loan was low. Wealthy persons could be persuaded to forfeit some of the interest, while older and less wealthy persons should by all means receive their due interest. There also should be stricter laws for debts and buying on credit.

Though Luther was aware that *Zinsskauf* was a legal form of trade, he knew that it was dangerous and contradicted natural law. It was also against the command of Christian love. It could easily endanger people so that they lost their property and ended in poverty. The only justification he saw was if both the person who loaned the money and the person who received it were involved in the gain as well as in the risk.

Luther was well aware that without buying and selling, and loaning money and receiving such loans, commerce could not exist. But the command to love God and the neighbor could not be compromised in business. Whether this needed to imply that one could not charge any interest on loans, as Luther preferred, must be questioned. There he based his rationale not just on the Bible,

---

41 Luther thought it better to ask for a tithe or a certain modest percentage of the actual yield that was gained with the loan. For elderly people and widows and orphans, he demanded loans without interest. John Calvin argued along similar lines but otherwise approved of charging interest, as was the custom in the cities.

especially the Old Testament, but on Aristotle. Yet his overarching view on economic matters is still worthy of serious consideration. He rejected an economy in which only a few get rich and opted for an economy oriented on the common good. He succinctly summarizes this in his explanation of the seventh commandment: "We are to fear and love God, so that we neither take our neighbors' money or property nor acquire them by using shoddy merchandise or crooked deals, but instead help them to improve and protect their property and income."[42] Caring and looking out for our neighbors' well-being without endangering our own must prevail in economic matters.

QUESTIONS FOR DISCUSSION

Why did early and medieval Christians take such a strong stand against charging interest on loans?
What was Luther's opposition to *Zinsskauf*?
What can today's debtor/creditor societies learn from Luther's teaching on usury?

---

42 Luther, *Small Catechism*, 353.

CHAPTER ELEVEN

The Christian Faith Is Not Hostile to Science

During a table talk of Luther on June 4 or 5, 1539, there was allegedly a conversation about a new astronomer who said that the earth and not the sky, the moon, and the sun were moving. Luther is said to have replied: "Whoever wants to be clever must agree with nothing that others esteem. . . . I believe the Holy Scripture, for Joshua commanded the sun to stand still and not the earth."[1] With this new astronomer Luther probably meant Copernicus, who marks the transition from the old, geocentric worldview to the heliocentric one. Luther was therefore a man of the Middle Ages and argued with the Bible against scientific progress.

But is this all true? The alleged table talk of 1539 was not printed until 1566 by Johann Goldschmied, called Aurifaber, and in the diaries of the contemporary witnesses present at that time, there is no statement by Luther on Copernicus or on progress in astronomy. Nor did Luther hinder the flourishing of the natural sciences at Wittenberg University. As physicist and historian of science Andreas Kleinert shows, Luther's having an anti-Copernican attitude was an

---

1 Martin Luther, table talk 4638 (*LW* 54:359). It is interesting that this table talk is titled "Luther Rejects the Copernican Cosmology."

invention of Catholic historians of the nineteenth century.[2] Franz
Beckmann and Franz Hippler, two Prussian Roman Catholic historians, were engaged in the *Kulturkampf* (the culture war of 1871–1878)
of the Catholic Church with the government under Prussian chancellor Otto von Bismarck (1815–1898).[3] They made Luther an opponent
of the scientific revolution of the sixteenth century. This historical lie
was then readily spread further by subsequent historians and theologians. In contrast to Philipp Melanchthon, who was a polyhistor,
Luther as a theologian had little interest in the natural sciences, as
long as they did not contradict his basic theological convictions. That
did not seem to be the case with the new worldview.

1. WITTENBERG'S INTEREST IN COPERNICUS

In his writing *Initia doctrinae physicae*, Melanchthon expressed
himself in detail on the heliocentric world view of Copernicus.[4]
He wrote that this supposedly new worldview was only a repetition
of what Greek astronomer and mathematician Aristarch of Samos
(ca. 319–ca. 230 BCE) had postulated in antiquity. Melanchthon,
on the other hand, cites Psalm 19:4–5: "In the heavens he [God] has
set a tent for the sun, which comes out like a bridegroom from his
wedding canopy, and like a strong man runs its course with joy."
Melanchthon thus referred to Scripture, which gave him a geocentric
view of the world.

Nicolaus Copernicus (1473–1543) himself was not interested in a
"Copernican turn" but in the development of a system that helped the

---

2 Andreas Kleinert, "Eine handgreifliche Geschichtslüge. Wie Martin
Luther zum Gegner des kopernicanischen Weltsystems gemacht wurde," in
Berichte zur Wissenschaftsgeschichte (July 2003), 26:101–11.

3 The Roman Catholic Church wanted to extend its influence on politics,
science, and culture, a move that was strongly opposed by the Prussian state.

4 The *Initia doctrinae physicae* (Introduction to Physics) was for a long
time a widely used textbook in Protestant countries and was published at least
twenty-two times from 1549–1600, occasionally revised.

classical concept of harmony of spheres to new splendor. As American theologian Harold Nebelsick (1925–1989) emphasizes, Copernicus "clearly had no intention of abstracting his geometry from the actual motions of the heavens as such."[5] At the time of Luther, people were still so strongly oriented toward the Greek idea of the harmony of spheres that Copernicus even sacrificed the accuracy of his observations for the desired elegance of his calculations. The church also held the prevailing opinion at the time and exhorted Galileo Galilei (1564–1642) to teach heliocentric theory only as a hypothesis and not as a fact. Only Johannes Kepler (1571–1630) pursued a path with his mathematics that revolutionized astronomy, because his understanding of harmony was supported by observation.

Luther was mainly concerned with the justifying word of God that was addressed to individuals. Since he emphasized the ambivalence of reason, it could not be a final support for faith. As Lutheran theologian Werner Elert (1885–1954) notes: "The church, which derives its mission from the Gospel and knows that the proclamation of the Gospel exhausts this mission, has no interest in the various world pictures." However, Elert goes on to explain, *"but that his [Luther's] theological authority hampered the spread of the new world picture is a palpable falsification of history."*[6] Unhindered by any theological interests, scientific representatives of the Copernican worldview were able to teach at Wittenberg University, and that in Luther's time. Even Giordano Bruno (1548–1600) was granted refuge in Wittenberg and taught there from 1586–1588. Since Luther was a theologian, there are no statements about the natural sciences in his main works. Remarks on astronomy come almost exclusively from Luther's table talks. Nevertheless, astronomy did not lead a shadowy existence in Wittenberg.

In 1532 Georg Joachim von Lauchen (1514–1574), called Rhaeticus, began his studies in Wittenberg. He studied mathematics,

---

5 Harold P. Nebelsick, *Circles of God: Theology and Science from the Greeks to Copernicus* (Edinburgh: Scottish Academic Press, 1985), 237.

6 Werner Elert, *The Structure of Lutheranism*, trans. Walter A. Hansen (St. Louis: Concordia, 1962), 1:423, 424.

which at that time included astronomy, and Greek with Melanch-thon. Melanchthon quickly recognized the talent of his student and promoted him to the best of his ability so that he got a professorship for mathematics, which also included astronomy. On a study trip that Melanchthon made possible for him, Rhaeticus visited Copernicus in 1538, with whom he stayed for two years. In 1541 he returned to Wittenberg, where he became dean of the faculty of humanities and a member of the faculty of theology. In May 1542 he traveled to Nuremberg to supervise the publication of the first edition of Copernicus's work *De revolutionibus orbium coelestium* at printer Johannes Petraeus. In order for it to be accepted by the theological side, Andreas Osiander (1498–1552), a good friend of Martin Luther, wrote a preface in which he described the theory of Copernicus as a pure hypothesis that just by chance coincided with the astronomi-cal calculations. This work was published shortly before the death of Copernicus in 1543.

2. SUPPORT OF THE NATURAL SCIENCES IN WITTENBERG

Elert writes,

> When in the year 1545 the professorship in lower mathematics had to be filled anew once more, the university, in its proposal to the elector with regard to an appointment, could point with pride to the fact that the universities of Tübingen, Leipzig, Greifswald and Rostock had fol-lowed the example of Wittenberg with respect to the encouragement of mathematics. Erasmus Reinhold, who lectured on higher mathematics and in whose company Luther observed the comet seen on January 13, 1538, also became an enthusiastic Copernican.[7]

Reinhold explicitly praised Copernicus and his work *De revolutioni-bus* and wrote a comment on it himself. Nevertheless, he rejected the heliocentric system for physical and theological reasons. It was

---

7 Elert, *Structure of Lutheranism* 1:425.

therefore possible to be a follower of Copernicus at the University of Wittenberg without having to fear ecclesiastical censorship. However, such a commitment to Copernicus did not mean, as we see with Reinhold, that one also shared his worldview. The scientific controversy surrounding the Copernican system thus lasted a very long time, even with ardent admirers of Copernicus. Overall, however, it can be said that Wittenberg was a good place for the promotion of the natural sciences, which is attributable on the one hand to Melanchthon and on the other hand also to Luther, who abstained from scientific judgments but showed a healthy curiosity about nature as God's creation, as we will also see in the next chapter.

QUESTIONS FOR DISCUSSION

Why is Luther erroneously remembered as an opponent of the Scientific Revolution?

With both classical Greek natural philosophy and the Bible indicating a geocentric model of the stars and planets, what motivated Copernicus to postulate his heliocentric model?

How should we understand the relationship between faith and natural science today?

CHAPTER TWELVE

Astrology Does Not Give Us a Glimpse into the Future

"The end of the 15th and the entire 16th century are considered the heyday of astrology. In no epoch has it been able to find such broad recognition and encompass such broad areas of daily life."[1] Even experts in the field of astronomy, such as famous Danish astronomer Tycho Brahe (1546–1601) and also Johannes Kepler, did not disdain to provide horoscopes. The popularity of astrology was partly due to the fact that it had a firm place in the curriculum of the universities. For example, a separate chair for astrology was established in Bologna. Further, calendars were widely distributed through printing, and an annual calendar also contained astrological data about the coming year, such as the expected weather, how the harvest would turn out, and what diseases and dangers of war threatened.

With this wide spread of astrology, it is not surprising that Philipp Melanchthon was also an avid promoter of astrological studies and had a horoscope created for his children immediately after their birth, just as his father had done for him. However, for Melanchthon the stars were only a sign of God's omnipotence, for they were instruments of his power, whose influence God could still change. The stars,

---

1 So Klaus Matthäus, "Astrologie II/2. Reformationszeit und Neuzeit," *TRE* 4:288.

then, did not exert any influence independent of God on humans and their environment, for the stars were subject to God's will and objects of his power and providence. That is why it was important for Melanchthon to foresee this will of God through astrology.[2]

For Luther, however, belief in the power of the stars was idolatry, which ran counter to the first commandment.[3] He rejected it as a limitation of God's omnipotence, for God alone was decisive for creation and its future. God did not need stars for this. Although Luther did not write on astrology, he often expressed his thoughts on astrology in his table talks. His comparison with Melanchthon is disarming when he says, "I believe that Philipp [Melanchthon] uses astrology, just as I take a strong drink of beer whenever I have gloomy thoughts."[4]

1. UNITY AND CONTRAST OF ASTRONOMY AND ASTROLOGY

Although in Luther's time every astronomer was also an astrologer, and therefore the terms *astronomer* and *astrologer* sometimes seem to be confused, for Luther astronomy belonged to the so-called exact sciences. He concludes from Genesis 15:5, where God says to Abraham, "Look toward heaven and count the stars," that astronomy is approved by God. Luther says: "Astronomy is the oldest science, and has brought with it many arts. It was very well known to the ancients, and especially to the Hebrews, who observed the course of heaven very carefully."[5] If it remains within its limits, astronomy, according to Luther, is a gift from God. However, if it predicts what will happen to everyone, that is, becomes astrology, then it is not to be approved.

---

2 See Stefano Caroti, "Melanchthon's Astrology," in *"Astrologi hallucinati"*: *Stars and the End of the World in Luther's Time*, ed. Paola Zambelli (Berlin: de Gruyter, 1986), 118–19.

3 Martin Luther, table talk 1026 (*WA TR* 1:519.3–4).

4 Luther, table talk 17 (1531; *WA TR* 1:7.9–10).

5 Luther, table talk 2730a (*WA TR* 2:619.12–14).

Luther admits, "I accept astronomy, and I like it for the sake of its manifold benefits."[6] Since astronomy was considered part of mathematics, Luther says, "I praise astronomy and mathematics that deal with evidence. I don't attribute anything to astrology."[7] Although Luther of course granted Scripture primacy over the knowledge of nature, he did not spark a religious war between the Bible and science. This was different from his confrontation with astrology, which he rejected for theological and rational reasons, without allowing a religious war to arise there as well.

2. THEOLOGICAL AND PRACTICAL OBJECTIONS TO ASTROLOGY

Most important are Luther's theological arguments against astrology. Commenting on Melanchthon's remark that people born after midnight under the sign of Libra are unhappy, Luther says, "Astrologers are very unhappy, who do not allow themselves to be imposed by God, but by the stars of suffering and trials; that's why they have no patience."[8] What happens comes from God and is not attributable to the stars. "Heaven does not ask for them, and our Lord God does not ask heaven either."[9] The divinity of God is also decisive for the stars, for God is the sovereign Lord of creation. The stars have no mediating function through which God would guide the destiny of our world. In addition, the future is reserved for God alone, so that it cannot be discerned by gazing at the stars. Also, according to Luther, one must not forget that the stars do not dominate us, but we dominate the stars, so we do not need to fear them. When Melanchthon announced misfortune for June and July 1532 due to the constellations of stars, Luther replied that astrology usually announces

---

6 Luther, table talk 855 (*WA TR* 1:421.21).
7 Luther, table talk 2413a (*WA TR* 2:457.24–25).
8 Luther, table talk 2952b (1533; *WA TR* 3:114.24–26).
9 Luther, table talk 4846 (July 1543; *WA TR* 4:543.12–13).

calamity, "whereas theology announces salvation."[10] When Psalm 19:1 says, "the heavens are telling the glory of God," then the stars should give us cause to praise God. According to Luther, astrology curtails the sole effectiveness and sovereignty of God and thus goes against the first commandment.

Apart from his theological arguments against astrology, Luther raises serious practical objections. First of all, astrology lives from generalities. Luther says:

> I have come so far and have brought astronomy [Luther actually means here *astrology*] so far that I believe it is nothing, although Philipp thinks that art is there, but you have no artists. They held this in the almanac as certain that one should not put snow in summer, nor thunder in winter; that you should sow in the spring and harvest in the autumn, the farmers probably know that too.[11]

Astrology, then is not logical, as he criticizes especially horoscopes that are created on the occasion of the birth of a child. If the rays of the stars already have such a power that they can determine the future of a newborn child, why not include in a horoscope the rays of all the stars that stood above the horizon at the birth of this child, instead of choosing only a few of them, Luther asks. In addition, he asks why the time of birth should be so decisive for the influence of the stars. If the stars have power to determine the future of a child, then "shouldn't the stars have influence in the uterus as well as outside of it? Do you mean to suggest that the stars care about a little skin on the woman's belly," and have to wait until the birth of a child with their influence?[12]

For many astrologers, even in Luther's time, the stars were still considered ancient deities who gained power over the future life at the birth of a child. For Luther, of course, this was downright blasphemous thinking. Luther also points to the opposite development of twins who were born practically at the same time. Thus he

---

10 Luther, table talk 1480 (1532; *WA TR* 2:109.20–22).
11 Luther, table talk 2892a (1533; *WA TR* 3:57.8).
12 Luther, table talk 5573 (spring 1543; *LW* 54:458).

says: "Esau and Jacob were born of one father and one mother, at one time, and under the same stars, and yet were of very contrary nature, place and intention. All in all, what happens of God and is his work should not be attributed to the stars."[13] Luther also refers to his own curriculum vitae to emphasize that astrology is not able to predict a truly concrete human life: "I have often talked about it with Philipp [Melanchthon], and I have properly told him my whole life how it happened one after the other and what I did. I am the son of a farmer, my father, grandfather, ancestor, were true farmers. . . . But the fact that I have become a baccalaureus, a magister, a monk, etc., that is not written in the stars."[14] In his objections to astrology, Luther also stood in a tradition, as is evident from his sermons on the Ten Commandments of 1516/17.[15] In addition to Augustine and British philosopher and theologian William of Ockham (ca. 1285–1347), this tradition that rejected astrology also includes Luther's own teacher at the Erfurt faculty, Judocus Trutveter (ca. 1460–1519).

However, one should not forget that Luther was also a child of his time. In a letter about the appearance of the comet later named after the astronomer Edmond Halley (1656–1742), he writes that it does not portend anything good. In a later letter, he adds that from the emperor and king Ferdinand bad things are threatening, because the comet turned its tail first to the north and then to the south. At the same time, he reprimands astrologers for pointing the power of the stars mostly to the negative, whereas there was one exception—the star the wise men saw—"because it points to the revelation of the Gospel, which is already present."[16] Klaus Lämmel writes,

> With this belief in the evil pre-meaning of comets and eclipses, Luther stands in a long tradition stemming from antiquity. . . . According to their assessment, these celestial events—as already in antiquity—belong in a series with "monstra" or "portenteta" of earthly origin,

---

13 Luther, table talk 855 (*WA TR* 1:420.23–26).

14 Luther, table talk 855 (*WA TR* 1:421.3–10).

15 Martin Luther, *Decem praecepta Wittenbergensi praedicata populo* (1518; *WA* 1:404.37–405.2).

16 Luther, table talk 2102 (1531; *WA TR* 2:322.14–15).

especially with monstrosities by birth, catastrophes in nature, or other abnormal or unusual occurrences that were inexplicable to science at the time.[17]

Especially in Luther's table talks and also in his letters, there are numerous comments about unusual occurrences in nature or with animals, which the Reformer repeatedly interprets as indications of the wrath of God and the near end of the world. According to Luther, God wants us to understand that a great accident or changes are imminent.[18] But here, too, he can again invoke Scripture, for according to Luke 21:25 Jesus says: "There will be signs in the sun, the moon, and the stars, and on earth distress among nations confused by the roaring of the sea and waves. People will faint for fear and foreboding of what is coming upon the world." Conversely, after the flood, God erected the rainbow as a sign of his peace with people. Thus, according to Luther, for whom the Bible was always decisive, these signs can be understood as God's warning to sinful humanity or as a sign of God's grace.

3. ASTROLOGY: A HUMAN ATTEMPT
TO FATHOM THE FUTURE

Astrology, however, does not start from the biblical message but strives to explore the future itself by interpreting the stars. Thus, the focus is no longer on God, who wants to communicate something to people, but on humans themselves, who want to seize the future. This is deeply contrary to Luther's understanding that God rules the world. Nevertheless, Luther found himself willing to provide a preface for the German translation of Johannes Lichtenberger's

---

17 Klaus Lämmel, "Luthers Verhältnis zu Astronomie und Astrologie (nach Äußerungen in Tischreden und Briefen)," in *Lutheriana. Zum 500. Geburtstag Martin Luthers von den Mitarbeitern der Weimarer Ausgabe*, ed. Gerhard Hammer und Karl-Heinz zur Mühlen (Vienna: Böhlau, 1984), 312.

18 See Martin Luther, *Deutung des Mönchkalbs zu Freyberg* (1523; WA 11:380.1–3).

prophecies, which were first published in Heidelberg in 1488. Lichtenberger (ca. 1440–1503) worked at German princely courts in the 1470s, and from 1473 to 1476 he even called himself court astrologer of Emperor Frederick III. His initially anonymously printed *Prognosticatio* (astrological prediction of the three stations up to the year 1576) "quickly became a phenomenal best seller, printed in more than thirty editions in several languages by 1530."[19] In this prophecy or prediction Lichtenberger had predicted severe tribulations, which extended especially to the spiritual and secular authorities. Since the spiritual and secular lords had become carefree and safe again after they had violently squelched the peasant uprising, Luther found this booklet suitable for awakening them with this threat of a heavy tribulation.

Luther makes it clear, however, that Lichtenberger's prophecies are not a spiritual revelation, because such a revelation happens without astrology, "but it is a heathen, ancient science that was of very glorious repute and widespread" in antiquity.[20] While God rules the world through his angels, God also "makes His signs in the heavens if a misfortune is to occur and causes shooting stars [i.e., comets] to appear, or sun and moon to darken, or some such other unusual manifestations to appear."[21] According to Luther, God threatens the wicked with such signs and warns them of future misfortune. From such events, astrology and the art of divination emerged. Since God's ways cannot be clearly discerned by us, this art is uncertain.

According to Luther, Lichtenberger's prophecies contain some truth, but his astrological art is uncertain. The signs in heaven and on earth are not wrong, as they are the work of God and the angels to warn the ungodly lords and lands. Making an art out of this is wrong, as can be seen from the fact that his prophecies have not

---

19 According to Robin B. Barnes, introduction to Luther's preface to Lichtenberger's *Prophecy* (*LW* 59:176).

20 Martin Luther, "Martin Luther's Preface to Johannes Lichtenberger's Prophecy: How This Prophecy and Ones Like It Should Be Understood" (1527; *LW* 59:180).

21 Martin Luther, "Martin Luther's Preface" (*LW* 59:182).

always come true. Moreover, it must not be forgotten that God did not make the stars to proclaim misfortune to us but "that they lighten the earth."[22] Although according to Luther the Bible points out that heavenly apparitions are signs of future events, it also forbids all prophesying with stars. Therefore, true Christians should not ask for such prophecies. For them, the statement Jeremiah 10:2 applies: "Do not learn the way of the nations, or be dismayed at the signs of the heavens; for the nations are dismayed at them." Luther also refers to this passage in his preface to Lichtenberger's prophecies.

Although Luther points to the end of the world in many of his statements, there is no connection between astrology and eschatology. One could rather speak of a connection between astrology and Luther's understanding of the law in the theological sense, because the extraordinary events in nature are intended to shake people up in their sinfulness. From astrological predictions there is no fear for Luther, but only from God. Yet he was sure that God was gracious to repentant sinners.

Ingetraut Ludolphy writes, "As soon as Scripture seemed to teach him differently than was otherwise generally accepted, he distanced himself from his contemporaries, even if they were the closest collaborators and friends. In doing so, he sometimes came to an attitude that surprises in its freedom from conceptions of time and that made him far ahead of his time."[23] He said of his close confidant and collaborator Philipp Melanchthon:

I regret that Philipp Melanchthon adheres so strongly to astrology. He's very much deluded for he's easily affected by signs in the sky and he is deceived by his own thoughts. He has often been mistaken, but he can't be dissuaded. Sometime ago when I came from Torgau feeling quite weak, he said that I was fated to die then. I was never willing to believe that he was so serious about this business. I don't fear celestial signs, for our creation is above all the stars and can't be subject to them,

22 Luther, table talk 678 (*WA TR* 1:322.15).

23 Ingetraut Ludolphy, "Luther über Astrologie," in . . . *und fragten nach Jesus. Beiträge aus Theologie, Kirche und Geschichte. Festschrift für Ernst Barnikol zum 70. Geburtstag* (Berlin: Evangelische Verlagsanstalt 1964), 175.

though our bodies may be. I'm not afraid of a chasm. I'll leave it to the clever philosophers to hold it in esteem.[24]

We see here the big difference between Luther and Melanchthon. For Luther, the stars had little to no influence on human life, and therefore there was no need to fear them, whereas Melanchthon, as a representative of Christian humanism, conceded that astrology was an important influence on human life. While Melanchthon never doubted the scientific accuracy of astrology, for Luther it was ambiguous and often wrong in its predictions. Despite these considerable differences in their assessments of astrology, there was no parting of ways. For Luther, the astrological interests of Melanchthon did not endanger the center of their common Christian faith, because the power of God was also for Melanchthon the cause for all natural and historical events. Thus, astrology ultimately points to God, who directs and rules everything. As long as astrology did not endanger the divinity of God, Luther saw no reason to intervene against it.

QUESTIONS FOR DISCUSSION

Why did Luther reject astrology?
How did astrology relate to astronomy in Luther's time?
Why is astrology still so popular today, despite our incredible advances in astronomy?

---

24 Luther, table talk 3520 (January 1537; *LW* 54:219–20), quoted in Ludolphy, "Luther und die Astrologie," 106.

CHAPTER THIRTEEN

Against Patriarchalism

Martin Luther lived in the late Middle Ages, an era marked by patriarchalism. However, one must not be deceived by this and conclude that women had no voice at that time. As Luther's marriage shows, his wife managed the finances and was responsible for the house and farm, including the servants. He, on the other hand, represented their house to the outside world. For example, his wife, Katy, once admonished him that she could not get by with the money at her disposal. He then approached the elector in order to achieve a salary increase. Luther told his wife in a table talk: "You can convince me of whatever you please. You have complete control. I concede to you the control of the household, provided my rights are preserved. Female government has never done any good."[1]

During his table talks with students and friends, Luther's wife sometimes listened in. When she raised her voice, Luther did not always appreciate it. As he once said: "Women by nature have the art of speech, which men have to acquire with great difficulty, but this is only true in the household; in the secular regiment, their oratory is of no use. That's what men are made for, not women."[2] For Luther, however, it was self-evident that the woman held an important

---

1 Luther, table talk 2847b (1532/33; *LW* 54:174).
2 Luther, table talk 1979 (1531; *WA TR* 2:286.13).

position in God's order. He said in a sermon of 1545: "For it is certain that nobody is born without a mother; but what is born comes from the mother. And just as Adam did not make himself, but was created by God; so all men must be created by God in the womb and there sustained and later be born with God's help into the world."[3] Without mothers, that is, without women, God does not create children and thus men. Women are the medium through which God creates children. That is why, according to Luther, marriage is the oldest station among all the other stations. He can also call it a "holy estate" and a "divine ordinance," because it presupposes "that God wants his creation and ordinance the holy estate of matrimony, to be maintained, in that little men and women are born and begin to grow up every day."[4] According to Luther, marriage thus serves first and foremost to maintain humanity.

1. THE STATION OF MARRIAGE

A man can thank God that he was created by God as a man, just as a woman can thank God that she was created as a woman, and both that they were placed in holy marriage to father children according to God's will and with God's blessing. Therefore, according to Luther, no one should hate or condemn this station and this order of God, but we should keep it high, dear, and worthy. Luther pointed out that at the time of the church fathers Augustine and Ambrose (339–397), every priest was still free to remain single or to marry. Luther opposed compulsory celibacy, which according to him was only introduced later on by the monks.[5] For Luther, therefore, the

---

3 Martin Luther, *Sermon Preached at the Marriage of Sigmund von Lindenau in Merseburg on Heb. 13.4*, August 4, 1545 (*LW* 51:359).

4 Luther, *Sermon Preached at the Marriage* (*LW* 51:358).

5 While during the first millennium of the church's history the vast majority of clergy were married, at the Synod of Ancyra, the modern-day Ankara, in 314 there was a first regulation prohibiting the marriage of already consecrated persons.

basic order of God was marriage. The pope, however, according to Luther, despised the holy marital status and considered it unclean. Luther thus pointed to the common belief of his time that monastic or priestly celibacy was more meritorious than marriage.

God created humans as men or as women, and therefore we should not turn ourselves from women to men or from men to women, but we should accept ourselves as God created us. Since we are creatures of God, we are to accept our respective bodily form as a gift of God, for "we are exactly as he created us: I a man and you a woman." From this follows the equal value of man and woman, for God "wills to have his excellent handiwork honored as his divine creation, and not despised. The man is not to despise or scoff at the woman or her body, nor the woman at the man. But each should honor the other's image and body as a divine and good creation that is well-pleasing unto God himself."[6]

According to Luther, marriage is a divine work that must not be prevented, because it is "a natural and necessary thing, that whatever is a man must have a woman, and whatever is a woman must have a man."[7] Of course, Luther does not miss Matthew 19:12, where Jesus speaks of eunuchs who are not suitable for marriage. But beyond that, there is no excuse to dismiss the station of marriage. Luther explicitly addresses the priests, monks, and nuns who have made a vow of celibacy, emphasizing that these vows contradict God's order of creation. But there are also those who, although suitable for marriage, remain willingly without marriage, so that they may proclaim the gospel and multiply spiritual children. Luther says realistically, "Such persons are rare, and not one in a thousand, for they are a special miracle of God."[8] Celibacy is only for very few, whereas marriage is intended as God's order for everyone.

Luther also knows how disdainfully the world can speak of marriage, for example that a woman is a necessary evil, and no house

---

6 Martin Luther, *The Estate of Marriage* (1522; *LW* 45:17–18).

7 Luther, *Estate of Marriage* (*LW* 45:18).

8 Luther, *Estate of Marriage* (*LW* 45:21).

is without such an evil, or that marriage is a short joy and a long displeasure. Luther, on the other hand, distinguishes between the estate of marriage and simply being married, saying: "He who is married but does not recognize the estate of marriage cannot continue wedlock without bitterness, drudgery and anguish; he will inevitably complain and blaspheme like the pagans and blind, irrational men. But he who recognizes the estate of marriage will find therein delight, love, and joy without end."[9] Marriage is God's work and pleases God well. When one recognizes this, one has peace in sorrow, pleasure in the midst of displeasure, joy in the midst of tribulation. We need to focus our feelings on God's work and on God's will, not on what we are looking for.

2. SEXUALITY AND LOVE

As we have seen, according to Luther, it is God's good will and work that humans appear in this world as men or as women. Since both sexes are good works of God, one should not seek to despise and belittle the other but honor the other as a good work that pleases God. God has ordered it in such a way that man and woman are dependent on each other. The inclination and desire for each other, that is, sexual love, is also a work of God. "And this is the Word of God, by whose power in man's body seed for fruit and the intense natural inclination to woman is created and maintained, which cannot be prevented either with vows or with laws, for it is God's Word and work."[10] This has been true since the beginning of creation and is still valid today. Luther speaks with high words of the love of the sexes, for it is the greatest and purest of all earthly love. He contrasts it not only with false love, which selfishly seeks its own, but also with the natural love between parents and children and among siblings.

---

9 Luther, *Estate of Marriage* (LW 45:38).

10 Martin Luther, *Christliche Schrift an W. Reißenbusch, sich in den ehelichen Stand zu begeben* (1525; WA 18:275.25–28).

"All other kinds of love seek something other than the loved one: this kind wants only to have the beloved's own self completely. If Adam had not fallen, the love of bride and groom would have been the loveliest thing."[11]

However, Adam fell, and with this fall humankind fell into sin. This also applies to sexual love, which is no longer pure. It is no longer pure devotion to the other but at the same time seeks one's own pleasure in the other. Even in procreation, carnal lust has been added. Luther follows here his mentor Augustine. He understands Psalm 51:5, "Indeed, I was born guilty, a sinner when my mother conceived me," as an indication of the biological transmission of original sin associated with the human act of procreation.[12] As a former Augustinian monk, Luther thus represents the Augustinian contempt of sexual pleasure, because for this church father sexual pleasure was sinful. But Luther also recognizes that there is a demonic aspect in the love of the sexes for each other, a selfish desire that only uses the other instead of loving and honoring one's spouse, as Luther suggests in the interpretation of the sixth commandment.[13] In the context of this problem caused by original sin, Luther understands marriage.

First, Luther clearly and unequivocally states that marriage was God's will and work even before the fall. It was not a stopgap solution to limit human sinfulness. God has instituted the marital station so that the world may be populated with people. Although for Luther marriage and children belong together as a matter of course, he does not see the meaning of marriage exhausted in the procreation of children. In our fallen world, for us as sinners, marriage also has the purpose of being a help and remedy against the licentiousness of the sexual urge and help against all the disorder that comes on us from sin. Marriage tames degenerate sexuality and curbs the damage to

---

11 Martin Luther, *A Sermon on the Estate of Marriage* (*LW* 44:9).

12 In OT exegesis today it is common practice to understand this verse as an interpretation of the historical fate of Israel. See Martin Luther, *Predigten des Jahres 1531* (*WA* 34/I:73.3–10), in wedding sermon on Heb 13:4, January 8[?] 1531.

13 See Luther, "The Sixth Commandment," in *Small Catechism*, 353.

body, property, honor, and friendship caused by an unbridled sexual life. Marriage can no longer be lived without sin, for sensual desire continues in marriage. Nevertheless, marriage is God's will and work; it is a sacred order that is under the blessing of God.

God does not hold accountable for their sensual desire in marriage those who are steadfast in faith and want to do God's will. The marital station, therefore, in spite of the sin attached to it, receives God's gracious word of creation, forgiveness, and justification, if not by nature then by God's grace. Even in sin, marriage remains a divine and holy station. Luther thus sees the love of the sexes through two lenses, that of God's good creation and of the behavior of humans burdened by sin.

According to Luther, marriage is the fundamental order of God, from which all other orders and stations are derived. It is commanded by God's creative will, since humans naturally have an urge to marriage. It therefore cannot simply be understood as God's commandment, but from creation it necessarily belongs to being a human being. According to Luther, those who do not enter into the marital station at some point inevitably fall into sexual licentiousness, fornication, or masturbation. These statements are colored by Luther's own experiences and observations with celibacy and contain a great deal of criticism of his own time.[14] That is why Luther can also claim that the one who eludes the marital station tempts God and does the will of Satan. Only in marriage is sexuality not a destructive power. That is why everyone should enter into marriage, if only because of the hardship and sinfulness of sexual life.

Luther, however, knows exceptions to marriage that are allowed by God. There are people who are by nature not suitable for marriage, and then others to whom God has given the high, supernatural gift of abstention so that they can remain chaste even without marriage. However, such people are very rare. They are "a special miracle of

---

14 This still holds true today, as we notice with the large number of cases of sexual misconduct in the Roman Catholic Church.

God."[15] The Roman Church ignored this, Luther says, when it made the law of celibacy for priests. However, if one has this gift from God, one may be grateful for it. But no one should dare to accept this abstention and strive for it unless God has specifically called one to celibacy or one feels empowered by God's gracious gift of abstention.

Luther thus concedes the possibility of a station without marriage and emphasizes its special task and dignity. While in the Old Testament it was sin to be without a wife and a child, this is no longer the case for the New Testament. Following Paul, Luther can even explain that the celibate state is better in that without the bond of marriage one "may better be able to preach and care for God's Word. . . . It is God's Word and the preaching which makes celibacy—such as that of Christ and Paul—better than the estate of marriage. In itself, however, it is far inferior."[16] This means that ethically speaking, there is no station higher than the marital one. Luther thus rejects the qualitative superiority of the priestly station. Through the burdens that God places on spouses, the marital station, according to Luther, also helps with the death of the old self and is the school of patient devotion in God's will. In marriage there are countless opportunities to show patience and love that an unmarried person does not have. Marriage is therefore the rule for Luther, but celibate life is the great exception.[17]

One should joyfully enter marriage and remain joyful in it, because one knows that God is pleased with it and with the spouses. The marital station is decorated and sanctified with God's word. Therefore, marriage is a powerful source of joy under all burdens, hardships, and disappointments. Marriage provides peace in suffering, pleasure in the midst of displeasure, joy in tribulation. "It is the highest art to look at this state according to God's Word, which

---

15 Luther, *Estate of Marriage* (*LW* 45:21).

16 Luther, *Estate of Marriage* (*LW* 45:47).

17 In contrast to today's situation, it was virtually impossible for a single person to maintain a single-person household. One was dependent on a larger household even as an adult.

alone makes both the state and the spouses lovely."[18] Luther thus rejects a secular view of marriage that considers marriage as only a human arrangement that has nothing to do with God. Marriage is holy by God's will and word.

3. MARRIAGE AS A WORLDLY AFFAIR

From a human point of view, however, the marital station can become holy only if it is lived in the knowledge that God has instituted it. This does not contradict the designation of marriage as an external, physical, or secular affair, just as Luther writes, "Weddings and the married estate are worldly affairs."[19] Marriage belongs to God's natural order of creation, not to Christ's order of salvation. That is why it is not a sacrament but an institution that is under the blessing of God. Even among non-Christians, it is a sacred station. However, since it falls under the natural order, the church is not responsible for marriage as a legal form. Marriage should not be subject to ecclesiastical legislation and jurisdiction but to the secular authority. Therefore, in the areas where the Lutheran Reformation was introduced, matrimonial jurisdiction was exercised by the secular authorities.[20] In some countries, such as the United States, pastors can obtain a license by the state to perform legal weddings. Then the secular and

---

18 Luther, *Predigten des Jahres 1531* (WA 34/I:67.5–7), wedding sermon on Heb 13:4.

19 Martin Luther, *A Marriage Booklet for Simple Pastors*, in Kolb and Wengert, *Book of Concord*, 367.

20 Because of the separation of church and state, there are two parts to a wedding: the wedding at the city hall, which has legal significance, and the optional church wedding. Since, according to Roman Catholic understanding, marriage is a sacrament and not a secular affair, the Catholic Church in Germany far into the twentieth century resisted the idea that the civil marriage had to be performed prior to the church wedding. Thus, it came again and again in strictly Catholic areas to church weddings before the civil marriage had taken place. According to the Lutheran understanding, the church wedding is a purely ecclesiastical act, by which the already legally married bridal couple asks for God's blessing for their marriage, which is bestowed on the couple by the pastor.

the spiritual aspects of a wedding are united. But in the United States a couple can also just be married by a judge or in Germany in the city hall, as became more and more the case in secular Germany, and forfeit God's blessing.[21]

Luther's understanding of marriage shows the consequences of the two-kingdoms doctrine. Marriage is a secular affair in terms of the order of creation and belongs to the kingdom to the left. It is not part of God's order of salvation, for one can be saved even without marriage. Thus, the question of what forms a marriage should take, such as patriarchal, partnership, or egalitarian, is one that must be solved in the secular sphere and to which the church cannot contribute with insights of its own. The form of marriage is determined by the respective temporal and social circumstances. This was also true of Luther's own marriage. As we saw above, according to the custom of the time, Katharina (Katy) Luther was responsible for the house, farm, and the finances of the family, while her husband pursued his duties in theology. Both were responsible for raising children: his wife usually during the day and when he was traveling, but he usually took care of them during family time and in cases of illness, although the children were also allowed to romp around his work table. There was no clear separation of the areas of responsibility with them, because in his long bachelor life he had learned, for instance, to mend his clothes himself, a habit he practiced during their marriage against the protest of his wife.

Although Luther as a pastor in public would have had nothing to do with marital problems, since the secular authorities exercised marital jurisdiction, he nevertheless took a position on certain questions when he was asked to advise a troubled conscience.

---

21 The church cannot establish any laws at all in matters of this natural order of God, any more than Christ and the apostles did, Luther explains. The only exception is where consciences are touched. Here it is the task of the pastor to advise and, if necessary, to comfort people when they are uncertain and confused in conscience or have violated the proper order of marriage. Luther often dealt with marital problems in his letters and in the table talks. In this respect he was a valued adviser.

As mentioned, he often dealt with marital problems in his letters. According to Luther, the real task of the ecclesiastical ministry concerning marriage was to proclaim God's will for a marriage and to proclaim the gospel to those who began a marriage. Then it should announce to them the power of faith and love, without which no marriage could be properly conducted.

4. THE PRACTICE OF MARRIAGE

Luther continued the traditional division of marriage into two parts. In front of the church door, the actual wedding ceremony took place, that is, the legal joining together of the couple, while in the church at the altar the spiritual act was carried out by proclaiming God's word about marriage, giving God's blessing and requesting the intercession of the congregation for the young couple. "When the parish priest blesses the bride and groom, he confirms their marriage and testifies that they have previously accepted each other and publicly confirmed this."[22] The so-called church wedding is thus even today, according to Lutheran understanding, only a confirmation of the previously consummated marriage and a subsequent church act of blessing. As aforementioned, in the United States a pastor obtains a license by the secular authorities to perform a legal wedding, and therefore the legal and the spiritual acts are intertwined unless a couple wants to be married by the judge only as the worldly authority.

Part of the essence of marriage is its publicity, since marriage is a public arrangement. Luther strictly ensured that marriages took place as a public act among witnesses in front of the congregation. According to Luther, a secret engagement does not give any certainty, and the statement of the two fiancées is not enough to recognize their marriage. Marriage should also not be conducted without the knowledge and will of the parents, otherwise one violates the fourth

---

22 Martin Luther, *Exempel, einen rechten christlichen Bischof zu weihen* (1542; *WA* 53:257.8–10).

commandment. On the other hand, parents should not force their children into marriage against their will and love, and parents should not disallow their children to marry if their child and partner love each other.

Marriage has a twofold meaning: the relationship of the spouses to each other and the task of procreating and raising children. Man and woman are first of all there for each other. The happiness of marriage lies in "that husband and wife cherish one another, become one, serve one another."[23] Sensual love alone is not enough, because it can soon cool down. Rather, marriage is a covenant of fidelity. "The whole basis and essence of marriage is that each gives himself or herself to the other, and they promise to remain faithful to each other and not give themselves to any other. By binding themselves to each other, and surrendering themselves to each other, the way is barred to the other body of anyone else."[24] In this covenant of fidelity, sexual life has a different context from outside marriage, because it is no longer determined by selfish pleasure but by the willingness to serve the other.

The physical union need not be limited to the procreation of children, but God allows the spouses to have intercourse beyond procreation as an expression and execution of conjugal love. Here Luther criticizes Paul when he writes, "Although Christian married folk should not permit themselves to be governed by their bodies in the passion of lust, as Paul writes to the Thessalonians [1 Thess 4:5], nevertheless each one must examine himself so that by his abstention he does not expose himself to the danger of fornication and other sins."[25] Conjugal love and fidelity prove themselves above all in the disappointment of the spouse, in conflicts, and when the other is sick, incompatible, or malicious.

Luther looks at marriage soberly and realizes that it is always endangered if it is lived only by its own strength. A Christian,

---

23 Luther, *Estate of Marriage* (LW 45:43).
24 Luther, *Sermon on the Estate of Marriage* (LW 44:10–11).
25 Luther, *Estate of Marriage* (LW 45:36).

however, does not superficially look at happiness but at God's will. Luther argues similarly when he speaks of the illness of a spouse. In this situation, one should not divorce the spouse but serve God in the sick person. "Blessed and twice blessed are you when you recognize such gift of grace and therefore serve your invalid [. . . spouse] for God's sake."[26] You can trust that God will not give you more to carry than you can bear. So it all depends on whether we enter into marriage with God or confidently, namely, without God, and stand in it. According to Luther, a first love or a temporary infatuation is not a viable basis for a marriage. "It's easy enough to get a wife, but to love her with constancy is difficult."[27] It is an act of the devil that one gets tired of the other and one casts one's eye on others. One should arm oneself against this danger by beginning and leading marriage under God's eyes and in prayer for God's help. Luther writes that although another woman may seem more beautiful and desirable to one than one's own, one says to oneself, "I have at home a much more beautiful jewelry with my spouse, so God has given me and decorated with his word before everyone else, whether she would not be beautiful or otherwise frail."[28]

The other aspect of marriage, according to God's word and will, is fertility. Here the mother is allowed to serve the loving will of God with his creature. She is dignified with her whole being to be an instrument and hand of God. This applies to pregnancy and also to childbirth in view of the hardship and danger of death, which Luther experienced very clearly on account of the medical and hygienic conditions at his time. What appears to the natural persons as a pure burden, narrowness, and hardship, the eye of faith recognizes as a unique calling to serve God's gracious will and to promote new life. God therefore calls parents as apostles, bishops, and pastors of their children.

---

26 Luther, *Estate of Marriage* (*LW* 45:35).

27 Luther, table talk 5524 (winter 1542/43; *LW* 54:444).

28 Luther, *Wochenpredigten über Mt 5–7* (1532; *WA* 32:372.18–21), sermon on Matt 5:27–29.

5. PARENTHOOD AND FAMILY

According to Luther, parents stand in God's place, and they are the highest authority on earth for their children. All other human authority, including that of secular authorities, is derived from parental authority. Parental authority extends over the secular and spiritual areas. Parents are the authorities of their children in secular matters. By virtue of the general priesthood, however, they are also the spiritual authority for their children and are obligated to proclaim to them the gospel. Therefore, parents should not only love their children and educate them for secular society and external success, but also give them the best in spiritual matters. Parents can attain eternal bliss through the good upbringing of their children or earn hell through neglect.

Luther would therefore have thought nothing of the opinion now often expressed that one should not influence one's children, that they should decide for themselves what they want to believe. Quite the opposite! Although Luther always emphasized that faith could not and should not be imposed on anyone, he knew about the role model function of parents and the truth of the proverb, "The apple does not fall far from the trunk." If parents do not have a positive relationship of faith, the children are also raised, consciously or unconsciously, to religious indifference. But God has appointed the parents as God's representatives. Therefore, children should look at their parents in God's place. This is how Luther writes in the *Small Catechism* that the children should honor their parents, because honoring is more than loving.[29] Honor also includes love and fear. Fear does not mean intimidation but respect. While love should not be without fear, fear should not be without love either, for both are to be offered to parents in the same way as to God. In order to properly appreciate the parent-child relationship, we must first bear in mind that the parents are the supreme, uniform authority for their

---

29 See Luther, "The Fourth Commandment," in *Small Catechism*, 864.

children. However, this authority is not based on any parental claim to power, for this is limited by the divine mandate of the parents.

Luther grants the father of the house extensive rights as head of the family. In addition to parents and children, a late medieval family also included house servants, journeymen, and apprentices of a craftsman or those who were simply fed there. In the relationship of the spouses to each other, the husband was superior to the wife, which Luther already deduced from the physical and mental disposition of the partners. But of the regular duties of the wife, none was under the dignity of the husband when necessity required it. In this way, Luther could describe how at night a husband would rock the baby, wash the diapers, care for his wife, and work for her, because this is pleasing to God.[30]

The wife is the partner of her husband. She exercises her laborious functions of the time—Luther was thinking of them here—in the house and in the garden and field under her own responsibility and not only on behalf of her husband. The rule of the father of the house is coordinated with that of his wife and is unrestricted in relation to the rest of the household. Although the household is subject to state law, its internal structure and the functions of its members among each other follow their own order according to creation. Therefore, the father of the house has his power neither from the state nor for him, but is independent of the state in the domestic sphere.

The main concern of the housewife is the economy. The father of the house, on the other hand, is responsible for the religious part of the family. According to Luther's preface to the *Large Catechism*, a father should go through the catechism material at least once a week with the children and servants.[31] Thus he has the same function for his house as the pastor for the community. The father of the house, similar to an ecclesiastical catechist, derives his mandate for the spiritual care not from an ecclesiastical commission but by his position, which as a baptized Christian is assigned to him by God

---

30 See Luther, *Estate of Marriage* (LW 45:40).
31 See Luther, preface to *Large Catechism*, 362.

within the family. As far as the promulgation of the Christian faith is concerned, this is by no means a matter primarily for women, as is unfortunately usually the case today.

The special function of the father of the house results from the fact that he cares for offspring together with the mother and that children are dependent on parental care, at least up to a certain age. The children thus have a similar relationship to their biological parents as people do to God, who created them all. Natural love for children, which arises from the biological context, corresponds to the will of the Creator. But it must not lead to carnal love, that is, to sexual abuse, because the parents educate for God and in God's place. Therefore, the parents should be concerned with the well-being of the souls of their children as well as the bodies of their children. Education for God, however, does not mean that the children should be sent to the monastery but that they are brought up in order to learn to serve God in service to others, in professional fulfillment and in readiness for church and secular authority.

According to Luther, the stubbornness of a child who resists the authority of parents is the precursor to the antisocial attitude of the adult and must therefore be prevented by wise education, and if needed also by also strict discipline. "With great zeal, children should be raised to a good fear, that they fear the things to be revered, and not to be made fearful in themselves, as is enough for some parents, so that they are very fearful, which harms them throughout their lives."[32] Unnecessary harshness toward children is foolish because it easily does the opposite of what the parents want to achieve. It is also a sin against the nature of the children, who in their naturalness are even closer to the original state of the first human beings than adults. Luther can therefore reprimand parents who do not want to come to terms with the natural childlikeness of their children or do not want to acknowledge their individuality.

---

32 Luther, *Decem praecepta Wittenbergensi praedicata populo* (*WA* 1:449.35–39), on the fourth commandment.

One recognizes in the relationship between parents and children and between the spouses a fundamental ethical, reciprocal relationship. Luther cannot be accused of a patriarchal understanding of the family in which the father was an unrestricted ruler, even if this was still common practice in his time. Of course, Luther proceeded from the superior position of the husband over the wife in the family, which was still considered natural for him and his time. This was justified by him from tradition and also from natural law. It is interesting that at that time, according to Saxon law—Luther lived in Electoral Saxony—a woman whose husband had died was given a guardian, who represented her affairs to the outside world. When Luther wrote his will, he consulted with lawyers. In his will, he appointed Katy as his sole inheritor and guardian of their underage children. This last will of Luther was extraordinary and contradicted the law of the time, according to which a guardian had to be appointed for the surviving wife and children. When Luther died, however, his will was not recognized, despite his reputation, and a guardian was assigned for his widow and children. However, Katy finally was able to regain responsibility for her children and permission that she could continue to stay in their house and manage their whole property herself. Completely against the custom of the time, Luther saw his wife as equal to him and wanted this to remain the case after his death.

The analogy Luther drew between parents and the secular authorities is no longer applicable today on account of our democratically constituted "authorities," even if we occasionally still speak of a "father of the country." While in this chapter the historical distance to Luther is evident, we should not overlook the modern-looking features in Luther's understanding of marriage and family. For example, the right of the parents had its limit in the first commandment, according to which one must obey God more than the parents. Luther joined the monastery against the express will of his father. As Luther's marriage shows, his wife had a free space in which he did not interfere as her husband. One can even speak of Luther's marriage as one based on partnership in the sense of a "intellectual and spiritual partnership of the wife,"[33] in which husband and wife depended on each other and paid attention to their common well-being.

QUESTIONS FOR DISCUSSION

How does Luther's view of marriage contrast with the earlier Christian traditions about celibacy?

For Luther, how is marriage both a sacred and a secular reality?

How is Luther's view of the family both similar and dissimilar to contemporary notions of family life?

---

33 So Ingetraut Ludolphy, "Frau VI. Reformationszeit," *TRE* 11:443, referring to Luther.

CHAPTER FOURTEEN

A Church Service Must
Be Joyful

In *Protestant Hymnal* (*Evangelische Gesangbuch*) of the Protestant Church in Germany, twenty-nine hymns are printed, to which Martin Luther contributed the text or at least part of the text. To sixteen of these he also wrote the melody. In addition, he contributed to two others only the melody. *Evangelical Lutheran Worship*, the hymnal of the Evangelical Lutheran Church of America, lists nineteen hymns for which Martin Luther wrote the lyrics, the melody, or both. If one imagines that Luther's hymns originated only incidentally, one has to wonder how many of today's hymns will still be in a hymnal in five hundred years from now to grasp Luther's influence on church hymns. Not surprisingly, in 1620 Jesuit Adam Conzenius wrote, "Luther's hymns killed more souls than his writings and lectures."[1] This means that Luther's hymns had a greater influence on people than his publishing activities and his sermons. They were even sung in the streets. It is no surprise that Luther came to music, because music education was part of the curriculum in school and at the university. However, it is not self-evident that Luther was musically gifted and interested.

---

1 Conzenius (1620), according to Karl Anton, *Luther und die Musik*, 8th ed. (Zwickau: Johannes Herrmann, 1928), 11.

1. LUTHER'S EDUCATION IN MUSIC

We do not know whether music was played in Luther's parental home. But already in 1497, at the age of thirteen, Luther attended the cathedral school in Magdeburg, which was led by the Brethren of the Common Life, a religious community founded in the Netherlands at the end of the fourteenth century. A year later he transferred to the School of St. George in Eisenach, named after the city saint St. George. Under Archbishop Ernest of Saxony (1464–1513), choral and figural music in the Magdeburg Cathedral flourished especially, and we may assume that Martin Luther also had to sing regularly in the choir.[2] He probably got singing lessons there and obtained at least part of his support by singing together with other young students outside houses.[3] Such begging for bread by students was common. In 1498 his father sent him to Eisenach, as they had relatives there, and he sang there again with other students in front of houses to earn some of his support. He lived with the patrician family Schalbe and was friends with the priest Johannes Braun (around 1450 to after 1516), who led a fairly joyful social life. In his house sacred and secular music was cultivated, and even motets were sung there. From 1501 on Luther studied at the Faculty of Arts of the University of Erfurt. At that time this was the largest German university, with about 260 new enrollments per year. As part of his studies, he had to acquire theoretical knowledge in music.[4] His curriculum included a lecture class on Aristotelian music. During his studies of the liberal arts, Luther was also active in lute playing, and at this time he learned to compose.[5]

After Luther had surprisingly entered the Erfurt monastery of the Augustinian hermits in 1510, the theological studies he soon began brought him back into contact with the musical perceptions

---

2 For the following see Joachim Stalmann, "Luther, Martin," in *Musik in Geschichte und Gegenwart* (2004), Personenteil, 11:636–54.

3 Brecht, *Martin Luther: His Road to the Reformation 1483–1521* 1:18.

4 So Brecht, *Martin Luther: His Road to the Reformation 1483–1521* 1:43.

5 Luther, table talk 6428 (*WA TR* 5:657.11–12).

of Augustine, Thomas Aquinas, Gabriel Biel, and others. He maintained a particularly close friendship with the cantor Johann Walter (1496–1570). When Elector Frederick the Wise died in 1525, his successor, John the Steadfast, wanted to abolish the cantor positions of Walter in Torgau and of two other cantors in Wittenberg. But Luther interceded vigorously for him with the elector.[6] Even as a family man, Luther sang with his baritone voice in the family circle and accompanied on the lute. The music director of the elector of Saxony, Konrad Rupff (ca. 1475–1530), and Johann Walter were guests of Luther in Wittenberg for three weeks in autumn 1525 to help him with the musical arrangement of the German Mass.[7]

Luther was friends with Munich composer Louis Senfl (ca. 1486–1543) and Thomas cantor and later councilor in Wittenberg, Georg Rhau (1488–1548). He also praised the compositions of Josquin des Prés (ca. 1450–1521), since he proclaimed the gospel through his music.[8] In 1531, Luther sent Senfl some books as a sign of gratitude for having sent him several motets.[9] Already the year before, when he was following the proceedings of the Reichstag in Augsburg from the fortress Coburg, he asked the Bavarian court musician Senfl to send him a polyphonic composition. Although he knew that the dukes of Bavaria were not sympathetic to him, Luther praised them "because they encourage and honor music so much."[10]

Luther also emphasizes in this letter to Senfl that music drives away the evil spirits and "that except for theology there is no art that could be put on the same level with music." Just like theology, music gives one a calm and cheerful mind. It was his conviction, as Luther emphasizes again and again, that music chases away sadness and

---

6 Martin Luther, "Luther an Joh. Walther," September 21, 1526, no. 1041 (*WA BR* 4:121.3–8).

7 See "Introduction to the German Mass and Order of Service" (*LW* 53:55).

8 So Brecht, *Martin Luther: Shaping and Defining the Reformation 1521–1532* 2:376.

9 Martin Luther, "An Hieronymus Baumgartner in Nuremberg" (January 1, 1531; *WA BR* 6:1.4–7).

10 Martin Luther, "To Louis Senfl," October 4, 1530 (*LW* 49:427–28).

melancholy. For him, theology and music are very closely connected, which the prophets already recognized, as they "proclaimed truth through Psalms and songs."[11] Music is therefore a means of proclamation, as we can see especially in Luther's hymn-writing. Music was also important to him for the education of his own children. When, for example, he sent his son Johannes to school in Torgau so that he should "be drilled in grammar and music," he expressly pointed out in a letter that Johann Walter, who held the position of cantor there, let his son "be instructed in music."[12] With this interest in music, it goes without saying that Luther put music at the service of his Reformation efforts.

2. LUTHER AND CHURCH HYMNS

Through the centuries, the faithful gathered for church services have largely been silent. In the liturgy the congregation spoke the *kyrie eleison* (Lord, have mercy) because it was appropriate, but otherwise the worshipping community remained silent. In the eleventh century the so-called *Leisen* (from: *eleison*) originated from the liturgical custom to allow the congregation to participate through Kyrie calls in the Litany of All Saints Day and in Latin hymns. The *Leisen* are short single-stanzas, usually four-line responsoric answers in the vernacular to hymns during the celebration of Mass. Since Luther selected several *Leisen* and expanded them to hymns, they are also regarded as precursors of Protestant hymns. Not surprisingly, Luther was not satisfied with the worship practice of his time. The congregation was not allowed to participate actively in the liturgy, except in the occasional speaking of the *kyrie eleison* or the singing of a *Leise*. In addition, the Mass was celebrated entirely in Latin. Even many priests did not understand the Latin they were reading, and so it was not surprising that the congregation had largely no idea what was going

---

11 Luther, "To Louis Senfl" (*LW* 49:427–28).

12 Martin Luther, "Letter to Marcus Crodel," August 26, 1542 (*LW* 50:231).

on in the service.[13] Luther was convinced that the congregation needed to understand the liturgy, including Scripture readings, sermons, and chants. That's why he first translated the Bible into German. People could now read the Bible for themselves. The next project was to encourage worshippers to actively participate in the church service.

In 1523 Luther wrote to Georg Spalatin, the secretary of his elector, "[Our] plan is to follow the example of the prophets and the ancient fathers of the church, and to compose psalms for the people [in the] vernacular, that is, spiritual songs, so that the Word of God may be among the people also in the form of music."[14] Luther was thus guided by the example of the prophets (psalm hymns) and the ancient church (Ambrose). As explained above, the Mass had become a show Mass in which the priest antiphonated alone with the choir. Since, according to Luther's understanding, every Christian is a priest, the Mass could not be left to the priest and the choir. When he thought of how to remedy this, he remembered the Ambrosian chant in rhyming hymns, which he preferred to the hymns in the Mass of Gregory the Great. Everyone should be allowed to sing along in the church. So he translated Latin hymns and had them sung in German by the congregation as chorales.

Luther also personally participated in the creation of hymns in the vernacular, which had a liturgical function in the church service and an advertising effect on the new faith in public. When in 1527 pastor Leonhard Kaiser was burned as a heretic in Upper Austria, he asked the surrounding people to sing "Come, Holy Ghost, God and Lord," which Luther had "improved in a Christian way" three years before.[15] Thus, singing became one of the most effective weapons

---

13 So it came to serious malapropisms. For example, the term *hocus-pocus*, according to a widely held theory, emerged from *hoc est corpus meum* (that is my body) at Mass. The faithful thought that the priest, like a magician, transformed the elements of bread and wine into the body and blood of Christ.

14 Martin Luther, "To George Spalatin," 1523 (*LW* 50:231).

15 Wolfgang Suppan†, "Reformation," in *Oesterreichisches Musiklexikon Online*, May 15, 2005, https://tinyurl.com/mrxcweup; *Evangelical Lutheran Worship*, 395.

of the Reformation. In the episcopal city of Hildesheim, therefore, in 1524 it was forbidden to sing on the street, and in Brunswick in 1526 journeymen shoemakers were reported to the priest because they sang Protestant hymns by themselves. In 1989, singing, which started in Protestant churches and continued into the streets, was also an important instrument for the peaceful revolution in the former communist German Democratic Republic.

During the Reformation, the faithful were fascinated by the idea of being able to get in touch with God singing in their own language. Luther's hymnal from 1529 is particularly instructive.[16] After a preface, Luther divides the hymnal into five parts. In the first part are twenty-eight hymns of Luther, twenty-four of which were written in 1523 and 1524 and distributed by song sheets. In Erfurt and Strasbourg they were immediately included in hymnals and liturgical books. The second part includes hymns written by authors with whom Luther worked closely. In the third part there are four medieval hymns, some of which were Germanized, namely, two Christmas carols, a hymn for vespers, and an Easter hymn, including "In dulci jubilo / Good Christian Friends, Rejoice" and "Christ Is Arisen."[17] In the fourth part, other spiritual hymns written by contemporaries follow. The fifth and final part contains fifteen cantica (i.e., biblical hymns), "Hymns from Holy Scripture, so the dear patriarchs and prophets made and sang ages ago."[18] Among them is the Magnificat, Mary's hymn of praise. This Wittenberg congregational hymnal from 1529, which Luther published, is the first illustrated hymnal ever, apart from the illuminated manuscripts of the Middle Ages. It is a book in which music, word, and illustration belong together. According to Luther, all arts are to be in the service of God, who gave and created them.

It is interesting that this hymnal appeared in 1529, because in the same year the *Prayer Book* (*Betbüchlein*) and the *Small Catechism* and

---

16 For the following see Markus Jenny, "Luthers Gesangbuch," in Junghans, *Leben und Werk Martin Luthers* 1:303–21.

17 *Evangelical Lutheran Worship*, hymns 288 and 372.

18 Quoted in Jenny, "Luthers Gesangbuch," 305.

the *Large Catechism* were published. Just as the *Prayer Book* was not only a collection of prayers but intended to introduce the Christian faith, the hymnal was not only a book through which one could acquire the hymns necessary for the liturgy but a comprehensive book of singing Christendom. The two catechisms were also not merely query books for teaching but introduced the practice of Christian existence. All these publications are illustrated. The Luther Bible is also illustrated. For Luther, word and illustration belong together, just as music belongs to it, and all three instruct in the Christian faith, more precisely in the Reformation faith. Practical theologian and specialist in Luther's hymns Markus Jenny (1924–2001) rightly writes: "The work on the hymnal is a self-evident and integral part of the congregational development, the necessity of which Luther became clear on the basis of the catastrophic visitation reports [of 1528]. It is therefore understandable that Luther could not and did not want to delegate the hymnal work to any 'expert,' but had to keep it in his own hands."[19]

Although Luther knew German spiritual hymns from his youth as well as Latin liturgical chants, he became a hymnwriter only when the Reformation was already well advanced. As usual, Luther acted out of necessity. He became a hymnwriter because there was a lack of suitable hymns. In 1523 he wrote:

> I also wish that we had as many songs as possible in the vernacular which the people could sing during mass, immediately after the gradual and also after the Sanctus and Agnus Dei. . . . But poets are wanting among us, or not yet known, who could compose evangelical and spiritual songs, as Paul calls them [Col 3:16], worthy to be used in the church of God.[20]

In order to revive the early Christian practice of congregational singing, he called for "German hymns that the people sing during Mass." In Wittenberg he was able to institute this, because in the

---

19 Jenny, "Luthers Gesangbuch," 321.

20 Martin Luther, *An Order of Mass and Communion for the Church at Wittenberg* (1523; LW 53:36).

Deutsche Messe (*German Mass*) from 1526, the German-language service in Wittenberg, German hymns were sung at the very beginning and after the reading of the epistle. The Gospel was followed by the hymn of faith, "We All Believe in One True God," and during the liturgy of the Lord's Supper, the congregation sang stanzas of hymns.[21] Although Luther wrote spiritual hymns even before his intended reform of the church service, his creations served "directly or indirectly for the proclamation of the Gospel."[22] In order for the congregation to actively participate in the church service and also to understand what was going on in the service, German hymns were needed.

German congregational hymns had existed since the twelfth century as a short sung verses, which were then followed by the *Kyrieleis*, the "Lord, have mercy on us." These abovementioned *Leisen* were sung during pilgrimages, processions, and other occasions, but rarely at Mass, that is, at Sunday services. Some of these one-stanza hymns were expanded to multistanza ones even before Luther, such as the Easter song "Christ Is Arisen." Latin hymns were also translated into German as early as the fourteenth century, and in Luther's time that was done by radical Reformer and revolutionary Thomas Müntzer.

It was important for Luther that both text and melody proclaimed the gospel. The melody was intended to reflect the joy of the gospel. Likewise, he did not forget the didactic moment. Luther created a series of catechism hymns, such as "These Are the Holy Ten Commandments," an arrangement of the creed, a hymn for baptism, or for the Lord's Prayer. Even children's songs were important to him, such as the Christmas carol "From Heaven Above." The first hymn Luther wrote that became known was written out of the deep impression made on him at the burning of two Reformation-minded

---

21 *Evangelical Lutheran Worship*, hymn 411.

22 Markus Jenny, "Luther als Liedschöpfer," in *Martin Luther und die Reformation in Deutschland. Ausstellung zum 500. Geburtstag Martin Luthers. Veranstaltet vom Germanischen Nationalmuseum in Nürnberg in Zusammenarbeit mit dem Verein für Reformationsgeschichte*, ed. Gerhard Bott (Frankfurt am Main: Insel, 1983), 294.

Augustinian monks at the stake in Brussels in July 1523. This song, which circulated on leaflets, was easy to memorize. One stanza of it reads:[23]

Two huge great fires they kindled then,
The boys they carried to them;
Great wonder seized on every man,
For with contempt they view them.
To all with joy they yielded quite,
With singing and God-praising;
The sophs had little appetite
For these new things so dazing.
Which God was thus revealing.
Must hear go gladly singing.

A genre of hymns that Luther himself invented was hymns of psalms. Before Luther, they existed neither in rudimentary nor in preliminary stages, but through him they "immediately had a tremendous broad effect."[24] Under this genre of songs falls Luther's most famous hymn, "A Mighty Fortress Is Our God," a rewrite of Psalm 46. The setting of this psalm is a hymn of consolation: Christ keeps the field, God's word overthrows the devil, and the kingdom of God remains to those with the proper faith. Luther also tried to encourage friends to translate psalms into hymn form so that they could be sung in worship. Strasbourg was the first place where his suggestion for the creation of hymns of psalms found open ears, and those hymns appeared there as early as 1524 for use in worship. Zwingli was also inspired to write a psalm hymn, and Nuremberg shoemaker poet Hans Sachs (1494–1576) published thirteen psalms in 1526. Calvin became acquainted with the German hymns of psalms in

---

23 "Luther's First Song: *Ein neues Lied* (1523)," Luther: A Site of the Antwerp Protestants, March 20, 2018, https://tinyurl.com/yzbs5py5.

24 So Markus Jenny, *Luther – Zwingli – Calvin in ihren Liedern* (Zürich: Theologischer Verlag Zürich, 1983), 18.

Strasbourg and was thus inspired to supervise the creation of the Genevan Psalter, which was first published in French in 1539 and gained wide acceptance.

Since the 1520s, pamphlets and hymnals reached the Austrian countries. In 1524, a hymnal was published in Tyrol that testifies to the Protestant spirit. As late as 1574, Andreas Franck published a hymnal in Graz, in which testimonies of Catholic and Protestant singing in church merge into each other. It was not until 1567, with the publication in Bautzen of *Spiritual Hymns and Psalms of the Ancient Apostolic Christian Churches of the Right and True Faith* (*Geistliche Lieder und Psalmen der alten apostolischen recht- und wahrgläubigen christlichen Kirchen*), that the new type of the hymnal of the Counter-Reformation was introduced. So one can rightly claim, "The Roman Catholic history of hymns and hymnals would not be comprehensible without knowledge of Luther's initial initiative."[25] This first comprehensive Roman Catholic church hymnal of the sixteenth century, published by the apostolic administrator for Lusatia, was clearly influenced by the Leipzig hymnal of 1545, which was printed by Valentin Bapst and for which Luther provided a preface. It is no exaggeration to say that Luther is the father of the Protestant hymns and the creator of the Protestant hymnal. His work provided lasting impulses for Protestant worship and piety far beyond Germany. Other denominations could not escape these impulses either.

For Luther, the hymnal was not only a liturgical book but also a house and school book. It was intended to promote the piety and faith of Christians in the church, at home and at school. Of course, music was an important school subject for Luther. Luther emphasizes: "You have to keep the music in school urgently. A schoolmaster must be able to sing, otherwise I won't look at him. You should also train young people in school [in this art] before you ordain them to preach."[26] According to Luther, school and church belonged together,

---

25 So Markus Jenny, "XI. Kirchenlied, Gesangbuch und Kirchenmusik," in Bott, *Martin Luther und die Reformation*, 293.

26 Luther, table talk 6248 (*WA TR* 5:557.19–21).

as it was a main concern of his Reformation to educate soul and intellect. In addition to the medieval monastic and cathedral schools, Latin city and council schools were established in the Reformation period, as well as German writing and reading schools. In the Latin schools, music lessons served to prepare students for liturgical service. The student choir was supplemented by a few adults and served also as a church choir. That is, school music and church music were largely identical.

Luther commissioned his friend Johann Walter to provide songs with figural movements. In 1524, as a result of this work, the first choral hymnal in the history of Protestant church music was published in Wittenberg, in which Luther's hymn "A Mighty Fortress Is Our God" could not be missing. Walter was then bassist of the electoral court orchestra in Torgau. When Frederick the Wise died in 1525, his successor, John the Steadfast, dissolved this orchestra, and after a few years without income Walter became a teacher at the Torgau City School. There he built up "the first Protestant church choir" and thus became, so to speak, the first Lutheran city choir master.[27] Luther wrote in the preface of the choral hymnal:

> And these songs were arranged in four parts to give the young—who should at any rate be trained in music and other fine arts—something to wean them away from love ballads and carnal songs and to teach them something of value in their place, thus combining the good with the pleasing, as it is proper for youth. Nor am I of the opinion that the gospel should destroy and blight all the arts, as some of the pseudo-religious claim. But I would like to see all the arts, especially music, used in the service of Him who gave and made them.[28]

The choral hymnal thus followed a didactic intention, namely, to lead young people away from lyrically questionable songs to good music.

In addition, Luther emphasizes in the preface that the gospel is not hostile to art but that art, and here especially music, must serve the

---

27 See Markus Jenny, "Johann Walter übertrug Luthers Musikanschauung in die Praxis," in Bott, *Martin Luther und die Reformation*, 321.

28 Martin Luther, "Preface to the Wittenberg Hymnal" (1524; *LW* 53:316).

God who gave and created it. To the honor and glory of God music and thus Luther's musical creations should be heard. Luther was by no means a purist, but, as already mentioned, he often picked up the lute at home and sang to it, together with his tablemates. For Luther, music was "a present and gift of God, not a human gift" that makes people happy and allows them forget all anger and other vices. So he confesses, "After theology I give the next place and the highest honor to music."[29] This brings us to the relationship between theology and music, which has so far only been addressed indirectly.

3. THEOLOGY AND MUSIC

Although Luther himself set hymns to music, his aim was not to give well-known hymns a different melody but to purify the text in accordance with the gospel. Singing was a hallmark of Lutherans from the very beginning and one of the most important instruments of the Reformation. Luther himself was a gifted musician who loved the harmony of voices and instruments. Unlike the Swiss reformers Zwingli and Calvin, Luther never spoke critically of music. On the contrary, he praises music as a glorious and divine gift of God that makes people happy. This should also be expressed in singing during church services. According to Luther, he was concerned "with changing the text, not the music." Luther did not want to become a musical innovator but wanted to reform the faith in accordance with the gospel. Thus, music should "serve her dear Creator and his Christians. He is thereby praised and honored and we are made better and stronger in faith when his holy Word is impressed on our hearts by sweet music."[30] Music served to spread the gospel and strengthen the right faith. He already said in his *Exposition of the Psalms* (1519–1521): "Once upon a time, music was

---

29 Luther, table talk 7034 (*WA TR* 6:348.20–24).
30 Martin Luther, "Preface to the Burial Hymns" (1542; *LW* 53:328).

sacred and divine. In the course of time, however, like everything else, it came into the service of pomp and lust." [31] Music must be changed from human self-expression to the service of God and of the gospel.

Luther sees a connection between music and theology, because music has a theological and a pastoral function. It induces a cheerful mind, drives away the devil, and contributes to the refreshment of humans. Luther also emphasizes, "The gift of language combined with the gift of song was only given to man to let him know that he should praise God with both word and music, namely, by proclaiming [the word of God] through music and by providing sweet melodies with words."[32] Human beings are given the language so that we can combine it with a melody to a song and praise God. This distinguishes us from all other creatures.

The close connection between word and song was also important for Luther's understanding of a worship service. Thus, in 1544, at the dedication of the castle church in Torgau, he emphasized that "the purpose of this new house may be such that nothing else may ever happen in it except that our dear Lord himself should speak to us through his holy Word and we respond to him through prayer and praise."[33] Speech alone is not the best form, because "the notes make the text come alive."[34] God himself also preached the gospel through music, Luther says, referring to Josquin de Prés, whose music Luther greatly appreciated and often sang at the table.[35] Although Luther did not reject Latin chants, it was important to him that people could sing along in their mother tongue in the church service. Decisive for him, however, was the word that was passed on through singing. For example, in 1542 he published funeral songs in Latin and German,

---

31 Luther, *Operations in Psalmos* (WA 5:98.38–40), on Ps 4.

32 Martin Luther, "Preface to Georg Rhau's symphoniae iucundae" (1538; *LW* 53:323–24).

33 Martin Luther, "Sermon to the Dedication of the Castle Church in Torgau," October 5, 1544 (*LW* 51:333).

34 Luther, table talk 2545b (1532; *WA TR* 2:518.6–7).

35 Luther, table talk 1258 (1531; *LW* 54:130n8).

whereby he also rewrote the Latin text.[36] Luther had a positive relationship with medieval Gregorian chant, as can be seen from the preface to the funeral songs of 1542. He writes:

> This is also why we have collected the fine music and songs which under the papacy were used at vigils, masses for the dead, and burials. Some fine examples of these we have printed in this booklet and we, or whoever is more gifted than we, will select more of them in the future. But we have adapted other texts to the music so that it may adorn our article of the resurrection, instead of purgatory with its torment and satisfaction which lets their dead neither sleep nor rest. The melodies and notes are precious. It would be pity to let them perish. But the texts and words are non-Christian and absurd. They deserve to perish.[37]

Luther praises the beautiful music and the songs of tradition, which he wants to take over even more of than printed in his booklet. However, since the text testifies to medieval and often unbiblical beliefs, such as purgatory, satisfaction for sins, and so on, it is incompatible with a Christian funeral and the hope of the resurrection. Therefore, this music must be cleaned lyrically. Luther emphasizes drastically: "And indeed, they also possess a lot of splendid, beautiful songs and music, especially in the cathedral and parish churches. But these are used to adorn all sorts of impure and idolatrous texts."[38]

Luther does not want textual or musical uniformity, for texts and melodies in all churches to be identical, because, as he thinks, different churches each have their own melodies and traditions. He admits, "I myself do not like to hear the notes in a responsory or other song changed from what I was accustomed to in my youth." For example, in the abovementioned *Christian Chants, Latin and German, for Burial* (*Christlichen Gesängen Lateinisch und Deutsch zum Begräbnis*, Wittenberg, 1542) he "provided not only German hymns, but first and foremost Latin responsories, with which he

---

36 So Markus Jenny, "Luther als Schöpfer des evangelischen Gesangbuches," in Bott, *Martin Luther und die Reformation*, 307.

37 Luther, "Preface to the Burial Hymns" (*LW* 53:327).

38 Luther, "Preface to the Burial Hymns" (*LW* 53:327).

unambiguously, audibly and consciously connects with the tradition, and further develops this work in the Protestant sense."[39] His general ambition, however, was not to leave the rich treasures of Latin chorale in the renewed church fallow. Luther thus granted tradition a certain right and did not want to curtail artistic freedom as long as the basic insights of the Reformation were preserved.

Thus, Luther's German hymns, that is, the hymns in the mother tongue, which were "tolerated by the Church until then, often rejected, less often promoted, are now an essential and integral part of the Reformation program."[40] They are sung a lot even outside the worship service, in the home and school, and are open to constant expansion, supplementation, and change. The Roman Catholic treasure trove of hymns was also greatly enriched by them. The noteworthy factor is centering on the facts of salvation history, not in the sense of an *imitatio*, an emphasizing or even an allegory, as was often found in medieval hymns. The focus became on praise and thanksgiving for what God has done for us and the encouragement of one's own active faith.

Luther's efforts to create music that corresponded to the gospel found their continuation in the cantatas, motets, oratorios, and passions of Johann Sebastian Bach (1685–1750) and the oratorios of George Frederic Handel (1685–1759). One year before Luther's death, in 1545 the most comprehensive Lutheran hymnal to date was published, which the Reformer had also provided with a preface, the aforementioned *Bapstsche Gesangbuch* (the hymnal published by Bapst), on which the Lutheran hymnal editions were based until the eighteenth century. It should be noted once again that this hymnal also inspired the Catholic Church to publish its own German hymnal.

---

39 Markus Jenny, "Sieben biblische Begräbnisgesänge," in Hammer and zu Mühlen, *Lutheriana*, 459.

40 So Gerhard Hahn, ed., *Martin Luther, Die deutschen geistlichen Lieder* (Tübingen: Max Niemeyer, 1967), xix.

QUESTIONS FOR DISCUSSION

What connection does Luther see between music and theology?
How did Luther's approach to hymns and liturgy influence
Christianity across denominations?
How should Christians today understand the relationship
between art and the gospel?

CHAPTER FIFTEEN

Martin Luther: Heretic, Saint, or Reformer?

When Luther died, all sorts of stories about his death spread among the old believers (*Altgläubige*), as those who remained with the old faith were called. For example, it was said that in his hour of death, he renounced his mistaken belief. Or Luther hung himself from his bedpost, and it smelled of sulfur, because the devil took his soul to hell. Roman Catholic priest Theobald Beer (1902–2000) wanted to convince me still in 1981, when I had accepted a call to a chair in Protestant theology at the University of Regensburg, that Luther was basically an atheist. Some arch-conservatives even today may put Luther in the heretic corner. But such views are strictly contradicted by the vast majority of Roman Catholic theologians.

Some thoughtful Roman Catholics will ask, Did Luther not divide the church, a division that we still suffer from today? Certainly, we still suffer today from the church split of the sixteenth century. However, it should not be forgotten that on July 16, 1054, Pope Leo IX pronounced a ban on the Greek Church, that is, the Orthodox, and since then the church has been divided into an Eastern and a Western church. After Jan Hus was burned at the Council of Constance in 1415, the Hussites rose up in Bohemia and from then on could no longer be completely forced under papal sovereignty. King

Henry VIII of England also broke away from Rome in 1534 with the Act of Supremacy and became the head of the Church of England throughout the world, that is, the Anglican Church. So did only Martin Luther divide the church? Or was he pushed out of the church by being outlawed, as it were? Until the end of his life, he suffered from the fact that the church, under the leadership of Rome, refused his reforms and slowly a new church emerged. He would never have allowed it to be named after him.

But there also is the anti-Semite Luther. Especially at the Reformation anniversary in 2017, there was a great deal said about Luther's atrocious remarks toward the Jews. Under National Socialism, these remarks were readily taken up by Julius Streicher (1885–1946) and other Nazi greats. But Luther's remarks, which are simply inexcusable, did not contribute anything to the justification of the absurd idea of a Nordic master race and the eradication of those defamed as inferior subhumans such as Slavs, Gypsies, and Jews. One should not overlook that with his remarks Luther also followed the trend of the time. As early as 1290, King Edward I expelled the Jews from England; in 1492 they lost Spain as their homeland, and in 1506 Lisbon. In 1517 even renowned humanist Erasmus of Rotterdam praised France for no longer being infected with Jews and half-Jews.[1] Finally, in 1519, cathedral preacher Balthasar Hubmaier (1480–1528) in Regensburg contributed to the expulsion of the Jews from this city and the construction of a church dedicated to St. Mary on the Jewish ghetto razed to the ground. The old Luther unfortunately parroted what others also let themselves be carried away with too. But in his earlier days he had good relations with Jews.

Although Luther certainly had his weaknesses, as can be seen in his often very aggressive remarks, he can hardly be described as a heretic. But falling to the other extreme and elevating him to sainthood might not do him justice either. As a Reformer, he held the saints in high esteem because they could serve as role models in

---

1 See Heiko Oberman, "Luthers Beziehungen zu den Juden. Ahnen und Geahndete," in Junghans, *Leben und Werk Martin Luthers* 1:519.

faith and in life. But they are not mediators between us and God; for this God sent us Jesus Christ alone. We can turn to him and to God the Father without mediation, as Jesus himself instructed us to do. But Luther as a saint? In no Lutheran church can the Reformer be seen with a halo. He was always aware that he was a human being like everyone else, with his weaknesses and strengths. So he did not grow up with the fixed idea of one day becoming the reformer of the church or of Germany. Quite the opposite!

Luther was vexed by the question that worried everyone at the time: How do I obtain a gracious God? Life was short. People hardly reached forty years because life was marked by hardships, deprivation, and diseases, against which one was usually helpless. If nothing positive was to be expected on earth, then by the grace of God one at least wanted to assure oneself of heavenly glory. In order to achieve this, foundations were established, all kinds of penitential exercises were carried out, and people, like Luther, entered the monastery. But Luther soon realized that even in the monastery he could not become what God wanted him to be, namely, a sinless and God-pleasing person. In the monastery, however, he was able to hold a Bible in his hands for the first time in his life and read it. The reading of sacred Scripture pointed him to Christ, in whom one could trust to be saved. It was impossible to achieve salvation by one's own efforts. In Christ, Luther recognized that God is not an avenging God who punishes us for our transgressions. Rather, God is a gracious God who accepts us like a loving Father if we fully rely on him. In Luther grew the knowledge of the grace of God, which is bestowed on us through Christ. But was this knowledge also conveyed in the church?

Roman Catholic theologian Norbert Greinacher (b. 1931) of the University of Tübingen writes:

> The Church of the 15th century was an institution that had distanced itself so far from its theological roots and its mission to the people that . . . there was very little left to recognize in it the "mission of Jesus." Rather, it was an institution characterized mainly by intrigue and power and wealth. The frightening descriptions of the era of the Renaissance papacy are well known, and at prince-episcopal courts and

in large abbeys . . . it was not much different. The Church had become a secular institution. . . . Individual outstanding personalities of this time, of whom the Catholic Church is rightly still proud today . . . , can unfortunately hardly brighten the overall picture.[2]

There must have been a reason why the educated people in the cities and also some rulers called for a reformation of the church at the head and limbs. In his *Church History of the Diocese of Regensburg* (*Kirchengeschichte des Bistums Regensburg*), Roman Catholic church historian Josef Staber (1912–1981) reports on Regensburg Prince-Bishop Pankraz von Sinzenhofen (bishop 1538–1548), who resided at the castle of Wörth, the summer residence of the Regensburg prince-bishops. Staber describes this bishop as a highly unfortunate choice, because in the time of the Reformation, when the Protestant faith spread rapidly within the diocese, an advocate of the Catholic faith with integrity would have been necessary. But Pankraz embodied the opposite: he unduly rewarded the cathedral capitularies who elected him with sinecures. "He was the father of a son, whom he had legitimized at the Regensburg Reichstag in 1541, and he was a sinecures hunter and, to make matters worse, also mentally ill."[3]

Luther also became more and more aware of these glaring problems of the church. In his naive way, however, he thought that the pope would certainly intervene against the abuses if he were aware of them. Only gradually did Luther realize that the pope was part of the problem and not its solution. Pope Alexander VI (pope 1492–1503) can at most be described as agnostic, and Julius II (1503–1513) did not have the nickname "the Terrible" for nothing, because he used the majority of his budget for warlike ventures. Nevertheless, he laid the foundation stone for St. Peter's Basilica in 1506 and was a patron of the arts, which he financed with the sale of indulgences. When Luther slowly became aware of these things, he increasingly

---

2 "Luther in Rom," Roma Culta, https://tinyurl.com/mt9b8xdj.

3 Josef Staber, *Kirchengeschichte des Bistums Regensburg* (Regensburg: Josef Habbel, 1966), 114.

took actions against them, based on his knowledge of the Bible as a theologian, and thus became a Reformer. What did he do?

As was customary in the late Renaissance period, Luther went back to the sources, which meant for him the return to the Bible. Since one can only be a Christian if one knows the Bible, he translated it into popular language. Since illiteracy was widespread, however, first one had to learn to read. Luther pushed ahead with an education offensive by expanding municipal educational institutions for boys and girls, because the latter in particular were largely excluded from education at the time. To understand the Christian faith, Luther created instructions for this, namely, the *Small Catechism* and *Large Catechism*, a prayer book and also a hymnal, because what one sings stays better in one's memory than if one just read it. He also took care of the education of the clergy, which was sorely wanting, as well as the worship service, in which the congregation could participate by singing together. But what does this have to do with the Roman Catholic Church and with other denominations?

Here one could refer to the saying, competition stimulates business. Decisive for this was the Council of Trent (1545–1563), which promulgated a strict demarcation from what was understood as concerns of the Reformation. For example, instead of going back to the Hebrew Old Testament and the Greek New Testament, as Luther did with the Bible, the Latin Vulgate was established as the source for the official teaching of the Roman Church. Similarly, in contrast to position of the Reformers, the number of sacraments was set at seven. The council also dealt extensively with the doctrine of justification, that is, the central point of the Reformation. In doing so, what was recognized as Reformation concerns were rejected, and the council put out its own position against them. These opposing positions have only slowly been overcome to this day. At the same time, attempts were made in Trent to abolish the most gross abuses, such as in peddling indulgences. The council also prohibited the accumulation of offices in the episcopate, so that one could not occupy several episcopal offices at the same time secured against appropriate payment. Seminaries were set up to improve the formation of priests. The duty to preach, which was so important to Luther as the proclamation of the word of God, was introduced. Celibacy also became mandatory, so that priests could no longer live in cohabitation. Finally, the Roman Catechism was introduced for teaching in the Christian faith, and a hymnal for worship. Most of these reforms were entirely in the spirit of Luther.

However, some of Luther's reforms did not take effect until the Second Vatican Council (1962–1965), for example upgrading the laity and noting that the lay apostolate is "participation in the salvific mission of the Church," or by emphasizing that ignorance of Scripture is "ignorance of Christ."[4] At the same time, the council went back behind the Latin Vulgate, which was established in the Council of Trent as the norm, to the Greek and Hebrew original texts of the Bible, demanding that "in cooperation with the separated brethren," that is, the Protestants, "suitable and correct translations are made into different languages, especially from the original texts of the sacred books."[5]

In this context, one must also recall the disputes over the Lord's Supper. During the Reformation period, it was crucial for Lutherans that the Lord's Supper was distributed to the faithful in both forms, that is, with bread and wine. On the old faithful (Catholic) side, only the wafer was served to the faithful, while bread *and* wine were reserved for the priest. But now it is also possible on the Roman Catholic side for the faithful to receive the Lord's Supper in both forms. Another point of contention at the Lord's Supper was the doctrine of transubstantiation. At the Fourth Lateran Council (1215) it was emphasized that through a properly ordained priest, the (invisible) substance of bread and wine is transformed into the body and blood of Christ. But the accidents, that is, the appearance of bread and wine, did not change. This was based on the philosophical

---

4 *Lumen gentium*, Churches (33), in Denzinger, *Compendium of Creeds*, no. 4159, p. 893; *Dei verbum*, Revelation (25), in Denzinger, *Compendium of Creeds*, no. 4232, p. 929.

5 *Dei verbum*, Revelation (22), in Denzinger, *Compendium of Creeds*, no. 4229, p. 928.

distinction between substance and accidents, which ultimately went back to Aristotle. In the ecumenical doctrinal discussions in the twentieth century, however, it was noticed that both the Catholic and the Lutheran sides were ultimately concerned that Christ is really present in bread and wine in the Lord's Supper, which the Lutherans made clear with the doctrine of real presence. Thus, on the Catholic side, one can now also speak of a *"trans-signification,"* but not necessarily of a transubstantiation.[6]

Thanks to the essential presence of Christ in the elements of bread and wine, a significant change is taking place in the elements. Here, too, one might say, Luther's understanding had a positive effect. Nevertheless, there is still a disagreement here, since according to the Catholic understanding, only a priest who stands in unity with his bishop and who in turn stands in unity with the bishop of Rome can celebrate a fully valid Eucharist. Naturally, this cannot be the case with Protestants. Perhaps in the future the view will prevail that the Lord's Supper is not a sacrament of a particular church but the Lord's Supper of Christ, and Christ does not divide but unites. Then this point of contention would also be resolved, and each could invite the other to the Lord's table.[7]

But Luther also had impulses that went beyond ecclesiastical concerns. Through his translation of the Bible, he was decisively involved in the development of the New High German language and enriched it with many expressions and proverbs. Through his emphatic assurance that everyone is called to a particular service and many other services for which one is responsible to God and one's neighbor, he fostered a professional ethos that can still be felt today.

---

6 Lehmann und Pannenberg, *Condemnations of the Reformation Era*, 99.

7 Of course, other Protestant denominations benefited from the growing consensus between Lutherans and Roman Catholics, as we noted with the joint agreement on the doctrine of justification. Moreover, virtually all Protestant denominations can be traced back to the concerns of Luther's Reformation. We have seen how Zwingli and Calvin were influenced by Luther. The same can be said centuries later of John Wesley, whose discovery of salvation by faith alone he owed to Luther.

Even the so-called Prussian civil service, which is characterized by efficiency, incorruptibility, and loyalty to the authority by which one is employed, can hardly be imagined without Luther's teaching of the profession. Likewise, so-called volunteer work, which is carried out as a service (to others), is rooted in Luther's understanding of service.

Who was Luther, and why is he also important for non-Lutherans? He was not a theologian of the importance of Thomas Aquinas. Rather, he was a Christian who stood in the tradition of Paul and Augustine, and in this tradition made the loving care of God, who is the Creator of the whole universe, to us humans shine anew. This salvational interest of God has inspired many people—consciously or unconsciously—to take interest in their fellow human beings, as we experienced exemplarily in the coronavirus crisis. The impulses that emanated from Luther not only are formative for Protestant Christianity to this day, but also revived and renewed the Roman Catholic confession to a degree that many are not aware of. In addition, Luther was extremely influential in German language and social life. So it was quite logical that the five hundredth anniversary of the publication of Luther's Ninety-Five Theses was not celebrated simply as a confessional event of Lutherans, because Luther's influence extends far beyond any one church. Luther belongs not only to Lutherans, even if they do not always rightly call themselves after him. He belongs first of all to us Christians and also to all those who are still inspired by his understanding of life being lived in service to others.

QUESTIONS FOR DISCUSSION

Having read *Luther for Everyone*, how do you assess Luther's complex legacy?

How should both Lutherans and non-Lutherans carry forward into today the salutary features of Luther's thought?

Selected Bibliography

Althaus, Paul. *The Ethics of Martin Luther*. Translated by Robert Schultz. Philadelphia: Fortress, 1972.

——. *The Theology of Martin Luther*. Translated by Robert Schultz. Philadelphia: Fortress, 1966.

Anttila, Miikka. *Luther's Theology of Music: Spiritual Beauty and Pleasure*. Berlin: de Gruyter, 2013.

Barth, Hans-Martin. *The Theology of Martin Luther: A Critical Assessment*. Minneapolis: Fortress, 2013.

Bayer, Oswald. *Martin Luther's Theology: A Contemporary Interpretation*. Translated by Thomas H. Trapp. Grand Rapids: Eerdmans, 2008.

Brecht, Martin. *Martin Luther: His Road to Reformation, 1483–1521*. Translated by James L. Schaaf. Philadelphia: Fortress, 1985.

——. *Martin Luther: Shaping and Defining the Reformation, 1521–1532*. Translated by James L. Schaaf. Minneapolis: Augsburg Fortress, 1990.

——. *Martin Luther: The Preservation of the Church, 1532–1546*. Translated by James L. Schaaf. Minneapolis: Augsburg Fortress, 1992.

Elert, Werner. *The Structure of Lutheranism: The Theology and Philosophy of Life of Lutheranism, Sixteenth and Seventeenth Centuries*. Vol. 1. Translated by Walter Hansen. St. Louis: Concordia, 1962, 1974.

Grane, Leif. *The Augsburg Confession: A Commentary*. Translated by John Rasmussen. Minneapolis: Augsburg, 1987.

Kittelson, James M. *Luther the Reformer: The Story of the Man and His Career*. Minneapolis: Augsburg, 1987.

Kolb, Robert, and Charles P. Arand. *The Genius of Luther's Theology: A Wittenberg Way of Thinking for the Contemporary Church*. Grand Rapids: Baker, 2008.

Kolb, Robert, Irene Dingel, and Lubomír Batka, eds. *Oxford Handbook of Martin Luther's Theology*. Oxford: Oxford University, 2014.

Lohse, Bernhard. *Martin Luther: An Introduction to His Life and Work*. Translated by Robert C. Schultz. Philadelphia: Fortress, 1986.

——. *Martin Luther's Theology: Its Historical and Systematic Development*. Translated by Roy A. Harrisville. London: T&T Clark, 1999.

Luther, Martin. *D. Martin Luthers Werke: Kritische Gesamtausgabe*.

McGrath, Alister E. *Luther's Theology of the Cross: Martin Luther's Theological Breakthrough*. 2nd ed. Malden, MA: Wiley-Blackwell, 2011.

Oberman, Heiko A. *Luther: Man between God and the Devil*. Translated by Eileen Walliser-Schwarzbart. New Haven: Yale University Press, 1986.

Pelikan, Jaroslav. *Obedient Rebels: Catholic Substance and Protestant Principle in Luther's Reformation*. New York: Harper & Row, 1964.

Stjerna, Kirsi I., and Brooks Schramm. *Martin Luther, the Bible, and the Jewish People*. Minneapolis: Fortress, 2012.

Wengert, Timothy J., gen. ed. *Dictionary of Luther and the Lutheran Traditions*. Grand Rapids: Baker Academic, 2017.

Wilson, Derek. *Out of the Storm: The Life and Legacy of Martin Luther*. London: Hutchinson, 2007.